FOR THE SAKE

OF ALL BEINGS

FROM THE WORKS OF

VENERABLE MASTER CHIN KUNG

For the latest edition, contact purelandpress@gmail.com
Edited by Venerable Wuling
Translations by Silent Voices and the Pure Land Translation
Team

15 14 13 12   1 2 3 4 5
ISBN: 978-0-9807114-7-9
National Library of Australia Cataloguing-in-Publication Data
Shi, Chin Kung
For the sake of all beings : from the works of Venerable
Master Chin Kung
1. Pure Land Buddhism — Doctrines. 2. Buddhism — Doctrines.
Includes index.
294.3926

Printed by:
Hong Kong Buddhist Education Foundation Ltd.
9-11F, Maxwell Centre, 39-41 Hankow Rd.
Tsim Sha Tsui, KLN, Hong Kong
T:(852) 2314 7099 F:(852) 2314 1929 E:amtbhk1@budaedu.org.hk

Printed in Taiwan by He Yu Publication House

CONTENTS

VENERABLE MASTER CHIN KUNG AM

Venerable Master Chin Kung AM (b. 1927) is an eminent monk in the Pure Land school of Mahayana Buddhism. He has learned Buddhism for sixty years and lectured on it for over fifty years. He is advisor to over 100 Amitabha Buddhist Societies and Pure Land Learning Centers worldwide, and founder of the Pure Land Learning College Association, Inc. (PLLCA), Toowoomba, Australia.

Master Chin Kung pioneered the use of the Internet and satellite television in propagating the Buddha's teachings. His recorded lectures are distributed in books and on DVDs, CDs, and other media. He has sponsored the printing and distribution of the Buddhist Canon and Buddhist sutras, books, and images as well as books on moral education. All these are freely distributed worldwide. To this day, the Master still teaches tirelessly on a daily basis. His lectures are broadcasted live via satellite television and the Internet to audiences around the world.

Born in Lujiang County, Anhui Province, China, the Master studied Buddhism and the classics under the guidance of Professor Fang Dongmei, a great philosopher of his time; Zhangjia Living Buddha, a renowned monk of the Tibetan Buddhist tradition; and Mr. Li Bingnan, a lay practitioner and master of Buddhism. In 1959, Master Chin Kung became a monk at Linji Temple in Yuanshan, Taipei and was given the Dharma name Chin Kung, which means "pure emptiness." He has served as instructor at the Tripitaka Institute at Shipu Temple, professor of the School of Philosophy at the Chinese Culture University, and president of the Chinese Buddhist College.

Master Chin Kung founded the Hwa Dzan Dharma Giving Association, the Hwa Dzan Buddhist Audio-Visual Library, and the Corporate Body of the Buddha Educational Foundation in Taiwan.

For his achievements in building interfaith harmony and fostering peace, Master Chin Kung has been awarded honorary doctorate degrees and professorships by the University of Queensland, Griffith University, and the University of Southern Queensland, Australia; and Syarif Hidayatullan State Islamic University, Indonesia. He is the Honorary Founding Patron of the Australian Centre for Peace and Conflict Studies at the University of Queensland.

In 2005, Master Chin Kung was appointed to the Member of the Order of Australia in the General Division by Queen Elizabeth II. He was recognized for service to the Buddhist community in Queensland, particularly through the propagation of Buddhism and the fostering of interfaith activities between diverse ethnic groups, and to the community through support for educational and health institutions.

In 2006, Master Chin Kung and the PLLCA were invited by UNESCO to co-organize the event "Celebrating the 2550th Birth Anniversary of the Buddha" at UNESCO Headquarters, Paris. The subject of the event was "Discover the Buddhist Contribution to Humanity" to enable more people to learn from the Buddha how to reconcile conflict and promote social stability and world peace through teaching. The goal was to prove that through the moral teachings of sages and saints, it is possible to teach people to be good, and it is possible to teach people of different faiths to live together harmoniously.

In 2009, Master Chin Kung was appointed as an International Trustee of *Religions for Peace* an international peace organization, which is active on every continent. Its mission is to create multi-religious partnerships to confront issues such as stopping war, ending poverty, and protecting the earth.

Since the late 1990's, Master Chin Kung has both initiated and participated in interfaith forums and summits in many countries speaking on the importance of education. He explains that it is imperative that all religious teachers sincerely "Learn to be a teacher and act as a role model for all" and encourages these teachers to practice the teachings of the sages and saints in their daily life, delve deeply into the teachings of their own religions, and also humbly learn from other religions.

Currently he is lecturing the *Infinite Life Sutra* hoping that the daily teachings can transform the current mindset of people today and help foster world peace.

Master Chin Kung's message of loving-kindness and compassion for all has been the central theme of his teaching. Harboring thoughts of sincerity, respect, humility, and harmony and dedication to help all beings to gain long-lasting happiness and joy has been his meaning of life.

FOREWORD

Rare it is to be born as a human.
Rare it is to be born
when the Buddhadharma is known.
Rare to have a wise Master to teach.
Rare to have the good fortune
to learn from the Master.

For over sixty years Venerable Master Chin Kung has been learning the Buddhadharma. For over fifty, with skillful means, great patience, and profound clarity—and the sincere wish that all beings awaken and find true happiness—Venerable Master Chin Kung has tirelessly taught all who wished to learn.

Countless gems of wisdom exist throughout all his talks, writing, and correspondence. The book that you are holding holds just a taste of them. A taste of the Buddhadharma for you to savor.

For us, his students, it was a privilege and an absolute joy to work on this book. Translations were carefully read and one excerpt after another seemed to step out of the files and into the book. The reading could have gone on much longer, from every translation that we have worked on since the early 1990s.

Unfortunately further reading would have meant delaying the printing of this book. That could not be allowed to happen.

And so, you now hold this first edition of excerpts from the ongoing work of Venerable Master Chin Kung.

Like working on this book, even titling the book was a pleasure. Upon asking some friends for thoughts on what to name the book, one replied, "What would sum up Venerable Master Chin Kung's teachings?" The answer immediately came to mind: for the sake of all beings. A file search quickly revealed that Teacher had indeed said that in one of the lectures.

Never has a title sprung forth so effortlessly, or so perfectly.

It is our plan to periodically update this book as new translations are done. Toward that end, if you feel that we have missed something, and we know we have, please email us the excerpt in both the Chinese and its English translation, plus the published source.

The Editor
Pure Land College Press
Toowoomba, Australia
September 2012

With deep appreciation

we thank our teacher

Venerable Master Chin Kung

who for over sixty years

has dedicated himself to learning Buddhism,

and who every day

dedicates himself anew to teaching

for the sake of all beings.

Pure Land

1. Purity, impartiality, and enlightenment are the guidelines for learning and practicing. What are we learning? We are learning to (1) cultivate a pure mind, (2) cultivate an impartial mind, and (3) be awakened and not deluded. Purity, impartiality, and enlightenment are three in one, one in three. The Pure Land school focuses on the cultivation of a pure mind. When the mind is pure, the land will be pure. The connection between us and Amitabha Buddha of the Western Pure Land lies in a pure mind. EILS

2. "Amitabha Buddha" is Sanskrit. Amitabha means "infinite," Buddha means "awakening." This name therefore implies infinite enlightenment. "Infinite" describes that which is innate in the true nature: infinite wisdom, infinite virtues and abilities, and infinite auspicious marks. These three categories of "infiniteness" cover all the infinities in the whole universe. "Amitabha Buddha" is a name of the true nature. That is why Master Zhongfeng said "My mind is Amitabha Buddha; Amitabha Buddha is my mind." ASC

3. To understand the cycle of birth and death, one must first know that life is filled with suffering, and that the suffering in future lifetimes will become even worse than in the current lifetime. If one does not want to be reborn in the human path, can this wish be fulfilled? Unless one mindfully chants the Buddha-name and seeks rebirth in the Western Pure Land, one's wish may not be fulfilled. Therefore, one must be determined to attain rebirth there in this lifetime. This is the true bodhi mind. EILS

4. With faith, vow, and the recitation of the name of Amitabha Buddha, we will be able to be reborn in the Pure Land and never again fall back in our practice. Up until now we have made progress in one lifetime only to fall back for lifetimes after that. This constant progression and retrogression is why it is taking us so long to attain enlightenment.

But once we are in the Pure Land, we will never fall back again, which will allow us to attain our goal much more quickly. And as we are progressing, we will learn the infinite ways in which we can help all those we have vowed to help be liberated from suffering as well. ASC

5. What is the nature of the mind? An example, which is easy to understand, is called purity of mind in the Pure Land school. When our minds are pure, all of our deeds will be good. Thus, we will accumulate far more than just ten thousand good deeds. Amitabha Buddha is a name of millions of virtues. As we gradually come to understand the true reality, we will realize that what Great Master Ouyi said was logical, that Amitabha Buddha encompasses all the infinite ways of practice. He said: "If we are able to be mindful of Amitabha Buddha, then we will understand all the wisdom of the Buddhist canon." CD

6. We Pure Land practitioners cannot make people practice the Pure Land method. When someone's condition has matured, we should voluntarily introduce Buddhism to help the person. There are many stages in learning Buddhism. As the person gradually advances in practice, he or she will naturally find the most direct route—the wondrous Pure Land method. Therefore, to help all beings skillfully and expediently, we should be patient. EILS

7. Amitabha's Pure Land is a land where saints and ordinary beings live together, but it includes all Four Lands. When we go there, of course we go to the Land of Common Residence of Ordinary Beings and Saints because we carry residual karmas.

In all other Buddha-lands of the ten directions, the Four Lands are separate. Sakyamuni Buddha's Land of Real Reward is in the Dharma Realm of the One Reality, and his Land of Expedient Liberation is in the four enlightened worlds. The lands are separate.

It is like schools in this world. Elementary schools, middle schools, and universities are separate. The Western Pure Land is unique. The students of elementary school, the students of middle school, the students of university, and post-graduate students all share the same classroom. This is unique. This is why it is called a teaching that is hard to believe.

When we go to the Western Pure Land, we are like elementary school students. But there are also university students, post-graduate students, and Ph. D. students in the same classroom. When we face difficulty, they will help us. An inconceivable world!

Therefore, attaining rebirth in the Land of Common Residence of Ordinary Beings and Saints, the

first of the four lands, is the same as attaining rebirth
in the Land of Expedient Liberation because arhats
are our fellow practitioners.

It is also the same as attaining rebirth in the Land
of Real Reward, the third of the four lands, because
bodhisattvas are there with us.

It is also the same as attaining rebirth in the Land
of Eternally Quiescent Light, the highest of the four
lands, because Buddhas are also there with us. ASC

8. Although there are an uncountable number of
methods, their objectives are the same. It is often said,
"all roads lead to Rome" and "all methods are the
same." Pure Land practitioners should never criticize
or slander Zen, Esoteric, or any other schools because
their objectives are the same as ours; they simply follow different methods. This is similar to our taking a
bus while others chose to walk. We cannot say that
they are wrong when all roads lead to the same destination. They have the freedom to choose their way.
BACW

9. At the core of the Pure Land teachings lies three
prerequisites, or guiding principles, for our rebirth

into the Western Pure Land: faith, vow, and practice. Faith is to have complete trust or confidence in someone or something. Vow is the vow to be reborn in the Western Pure Land. Practice is reciting the Buddha-name as well as living a moral life.

As Great Master Ouyi wrote in his commentary on the Amitabha Sutra, "Without faith, we are not sufficiently equipped to take vows. Without vows, we are not sufficiently equipped to guide our practice. Without the wondrous practice of reciting the Buddha-name, we are not sufficiently equipped to fulfill our vows and to bring our faith to fruition." ASC

10. Sentient beings are deluded. They indulge in the Five Desires and the Six Dusts—in worldly pleasures. We should generate a mind of great compassion, empathize with sentient beings, and introduce the Pure Land method to them. Compassion and empathy must be put into action. This is enthusiastically propagating the Pure Land method. With all our hearts, we must do our best—we must treat this task as the most important thing in this lifetime. EILS

11. Mr. Li Bingnan often said that only two or three out of ten thousand Pure Land practitioners are able to actually attain rebirth. It is because these two or three practitioners truly believe, accept and practice—the others do not. These 9997 practitioners chant with their mouths only and are not mindful in their chanting. They have not eliminated their afflictions and residual habits. They are still attached to fame, prestige, gain, wealth, the Five Desires, and the Six Dusts. When this is the case, even Buddhas cannot do anything about it. ASC

12. Those who can accept the Pure Land method possess great roots of goodness, good fortune, and good causes and conditions. If we did not already have the best root nature, it would be impossible for us to accept the Buddha Mindfulness Chanting method. Those, who can accept it and practice earnestly, can neutralize the transgressions accumulated over infinite lifetimes with the merits of their chanting.

The Pure Land is a gathering place for the utmost virtuous people. Once reborn there, we will be a member of this assembly and the equal of such virtuous people as the Bodhisattvas Samantabhadra,

Manjusri, Avalokiteshvara, and Mahasthamaprapta.
CD

13. We should put into practice Great Master Yinguang's teaching of "maintaining the five [human] relationships, faithfully fulfilling one's responsibilities,
avoiding being polluted by that which is bad, keeping
a respectful and sincere mindset, believing in and
vowing to practice the Buddha-name chanting
method, and aspiring to attain rebirth in the Western
Pure Land." This is the absolute direction and the
only goal. ASC

14. The causes and conditions of how the Land of Ultimate Bliss came about were different from those for
the other Buddha Lands. The causes and conditions
for the latter were complicated and not simple: good
ones and bad ones were mixed together. In the Western Pure Land, Dharmakara chose only pure and virtuous dharmas. His purpose was to provide a wonderful learning and practice environment for the beings
from all the Buddha Lands in the ten directions who
truly generate the great mind and who aspire to [un-
derstand and] transcend the cycle of birth and death,

and attain Buddhahood in one lifetime. He wanted to provide the best learning and living environment. EILS

15. Having good roots means that we have firm belief and firm vows. We have firm belief when we do not have the slightest doubt about the Pure Land teachings. We have firm vows when our one and only wish is to attain rebirth in the Land of Ultimate Bliss, and we let go of everything in this world except this wish. We must have these two conditions to be considered as having good roots. ASC

16. Great Master Yinguang spoke of small-size cultivation centers with no more than twenty practitioners. Small centers will be easy to maintain. There is no need to ask for donations, no need to hold Dharma assemblies or ceremonies for helping the deceased attain a better rebirth, and no need to confer precepts or to give lectures on the sutras. . . .

But it is hard to find practitioners of the same mind. Pure Land learning centers could completely follow Great Master Yinguang's instruction, but I added one thing: a lecture session. Why? Because if we do not understand the Pure Land teachings, we may gradually lose our enthusiasm. The more we listen to lectures on the sutras, the more we will understand the Pure Land teachings. Listening to lectures on the sutras will help us dissolve our doubts, develop confidence, and strengthen our belief and vow. It will guarantee our success in this lifetime. We should do nothing else but listen to lectures on the sutras and mindfully chant "Amituofo." In so doing, our minds will always be focused. ASC

17. When the Buddha was in this world, which was during the Dharma-perfect Age, people had high capacities and the majority could succeed in any method that they chose to practice! After the Buddha's time, during the Dharma-semblance Age, people did not have as high a capacity as earlier. With that, the quality of the Buddha's teachings gradually deteriorated as it was passed down. But it was not that the sutras had degenerated; rather, it was the lecturers' interpretation of the sutras that had worsened. As time went by, the lectures on the Dharma became more and more incorrect.

Now it is the Dharma-ending Age, more than three thousand years after the Buddha's parinirvana. The deterioration has reached a point where we do not know what to do. It gets more and more difficult for us to attain realization from learning and practicing Buddhism. EILS

18. It is said in Buddhism that "nothing can be carried over to the next life except our karma." These are critical words of caution. Knowing that our karma will follow us like a shadow, we need to be diligent in cultivating good deeds and not to carry our negative karma with us, for to do so will lead us in the Three Bad Paths. Good karma will lead us to be reborn in the Three Good Paths. And pure karma from Constant Mindfulness of Buddha Amitabha will lead us to be reborn in the Western Pure Land.

From this, it is clear what we need to do in this life. We need to broaden our perceptions and expand our thinking instead of being concerned with trivialities or calculating our gains and losses. Life is very short. It would be of tremendous merit if we could do more goodness in this life, to benefit more people. CD

19. Three thousand years ago, the Buddha knew completely what was going to happen in society today! He did not fail those of us who truly sought transcendence, who truly sought enlightenment. In the *Great Collection Sutra*, he said that in the Dharma-perfect Age, one could succeed in cultivation by observing the precepts; in the Dharma-semblance Age, one could succeed in cultivation by practicing meditative concentration; and in the Dharma-ending Age, one could succeed in cultivation by learning the Pure Land method.

The Buddha was telling us, the people today, that we will definitely succeed in our cultivation if we learn and practice the Pure Land method. EILS

20. The most important thing in our cultivation is to correct our wrong behavior. If we are not happy with a person or a thing, it will obstruct our rebirth in the Land of Ultimate Bliss, because our minds are not pure. This is why it is hard to attain rebirth in the Land of Ultimate Bliss and why Mr. Li Bingnan said that only one or two out of ten thousand Pure Land practitioners succeed in attaining rebirth there. Most practitioners only manage to suppress, not eradicate,

their afflictions. It depends entirely on their luck when they are on deathbed. If they cannot suppress their afflictions that arise at the moment of their last breath, they will fall into the Three Evil Paths. ASC

21. The Western Pure Land is an ultimate, perfect state. If a person wants to learn a particular method, this person, whatever his capacity, will hear the method that accords with his or her capacity. For example, if one has the capacity for Theravada teachings, one will hear Buddhas and bodhisattvas lecturing on Theravada teachings. If one has the capacity for Mahayana teachings, one will hear nothing but Mahayana teachings. A being will immediately hear what he or she wants to hear, and immediately see what he or she wants to see—all at the level of the being's capacity. This is great perfection and truly ultimate. EILS

22. There are two ways to be reborn into the Pure Land. One way is to cultivate and accumulate merits and virtues daily, and to follow the regular way of practice to seek rebirth into the Pure Land. The other way is for those who have committed egregious evil

deeds to be deeply remorseful at the last moments of their life.

Therefore, do not look down on those who have committed wrongdoings. Perhaps at the last moment of their lives, their ability to feel deep remorse will be so strong that they may attain a higher level of rebirth than we can. This is very possible. It is said that a prodigal who returns home is more precious than gold. Ordinary people cannot be compared with them. Thus, we cannot look down on those who have committed wrongdoings. CD

23. The bodhisattvas of the Western Pure Land have the ability to travel to all the Buddha Lands and to any place in the entire Dharma Realm. The sutras teach that the past has no beginning and the future has no end. From this, we know that space (in Buddhism it is called Dharma Realm) is immensely vast. This is the area the bodhisattvas cover in their travels — the vastness of the Dharma Realm. If they have an affinity with a place, they will manifest themselves there to benefit the beings. EILS

24. Like Sakyamuni Buddha, all Buddhas lecture according to the level of the audience. When the people in the audience have different capacities, there are many sutras that the Buddhas would not speak. But they would definitely speak the three Pure Land sutras. Why? Because these sutras are suitable for all beings. These are the sutras that all Buddhas must speak. That is, they must introduce the Pure Land teachings to all beings. If a being's conditions have matured, and this being believes, makes the vow, and practices the teachings, he will make accomplishment in this life. And the great vow of all Buddhas to help all beings will be fulfilled. ASC

25. The conditions are mature for some beings but not for others. If a being does not have the conditions, one should help the being develop the conditions. If the conditions of a being are not yet mature, one should help them mature. If the conditions of a being have matured, one should guide that being to attain rebirth in the Western Pure Land. EILS

26. Throughout the boundless worlds in the ten directions, the bodhisattvas of the Land of Ultimate Bliss

(1) seek the Buddhadharma and (2) help all beings. When they seek the Buddhadharma, they are not attached to the act of seeking. When they help beings, they are not attached to the act of helping. They discard all attachments and teach all beings. This way, they are able to attain infinite merits and virtues. EILS

27. As Pure Land practitioners, we have to achieve a certain level of attainment and transcend the cycle of rebirth to be able to be reborn into the Western Pure Land. Theravada practitioners need to reach, at the least, the level of Stream-enterer, which is achieved by severing various wrong views. It is the lowest of the four stages of sagehood in Theravada Buddhism. At this point of attainment, practitioners will continue to be reborn into the heaven and human realms for seven more times. In this way, they are assured of attaining the state of arhat although it may take them a long time to do so. But by not falling into the Three Bad Realms, they are considered to have achieved attainment.

According to this criterion, the minimum standard to achieve attainment in Mahayana Buddhism is to rid ourselves of a portion of our attachments, to sever the eighty-eight kinds of deviated thoughts and views. If we cannot sever these, we have not yet achieved attainment. Mahayana practitioners, who successfully sever them, reach the Initial Belief Stage. Theravada practitioners who sever various wrong views reach the stage of Stream-enterer. Without these accomplishments, we will still be reincarnating within the cycle of rebirth, still repaying our debts.

However, there is still another way: to seek rebirth in the Western Pure Land. Otherwise, attainment is not possible. If we cannot go to the Pure Land, we will have achieved nothing. Seeking rebirth in the Pure Land is actually much simpler than severing the eighty-eight kinds of improper thoughts and views because we do not need to sever them all, but can carry our remaining karma with us. As long as we have faith, vows, and practice [moral living and constant mindfulness of Amitabha Buddha], we will achieve attainment. The Buddha explained this to us in the *Infinite Life Sutra* and the *Amitabha Sutra*. CD

28. If we can discard all wandering thoughts and attachments, we will attain infinite merits and virtues. If there is even one thing that we cannot discard or let

go of, we will not have any achievement. But to let go is truly hard. Because of this, infinite great compassion arose in Amitabha Buddha, and he established a special cultivation place in the Dharma Realm for learning and practice—for beings like us who cannot let go to also have achievement. This is inconceivable!

With the cultivation places of all the other Buddhas in the ten directions, one must let go of both worldly phenomena and supramundane teachings before one can be reborn there. But, only in the land of Amitabha Buddha, [while letting go is ideal,] not letting go is also alright. This way, everyone will be truly helped and awakened. EILS

29. What if we can truly put down all the wandering thoughts, discriminations, and attachments? The world will be changed immediately! What will it become? The world will become the Land of Ultimate Bliss. What is the difference between our land and the Land of Ultimate Bliss? Sakyamuni Buddha introduced us to the Land of Ultimate Bliss where people of supreme virtue assemble. When people's minds are virtuous, the land will be stable and secure. Everything will be wonderful, without the least defect.

When people's minds are vicious, the land and every-thing in it will be vicious too. WPH

30. People with true aspiration and profound insight need to know that seeking rebirth into the Pure Land wholeheartedly and meeting Amitabha Buddha is the perfect and complete accomplishment of life. We should let go of attachments to worldly activities, both physical and mental, and rid ourselves of differentiating thoughts. There is nothing worthy of worry and nothing worthy of greed. We accord with conditions and do not seek affinities in our daily lives. How happy and free we will be for we will have truly achieved. CD

31. This world does not provide a good learning environment nor does it provide good teachers or fellow practitioners. The human life span is short, far too short for learning. Amitabha Buddha provides us with the best learning environment. And if we want to go, we can. Sakyamuni Buddha told us that when we go to that environment, all Buddhas will be our teachers, and people of supreme virtue will be our fellow practitioners. ASC

32. In the Pure Land there is no cause for our greed, anger, and ignorance to arise. Why? Because whatever we need will appear before us, so we have no cause to become greedy. Everyone in the Western Pure Land is a good person. Nobody has any bad thoughts or bad intentions. Nobody uses harsh language. We have no cause to become angry. In other words, there is no condition for us to become angry.

What our senses touch is the Dharma, the sages' teachings. We will not be ignorant. In other words, we do not have to end or do anything about our greed, anger, and ignorance. When we live there long enough, our greed, anger, and ignorance will naturally be uprooted. ASC

33. If one does not have the Ten Virtuous Karmas as a foundation for one's learning and practice, one will not be able to attain rebirth in the Western Pure Land even though one practices Buddha-name chanting. How do we know this?

It is stated in the *Visualization Sutra* that one should first cultivate the Three Conditions before [beginning to] cultivate the pure karma to go to the Pure Land. The Three Conditions are the foundation of

Mahayana Buddhism. Without such foundation, one will not succeed in one's cultivation and learning, regardless of which Dharma door one learns and practices. The Three Conditions are the common foundation. They are "the true causes—the pure karmas—that the Buddhas of the three time periods cultivate to attain Buddhahood." The three time periods refer to the past, the present, and the future.

There are innumerable Dharma doors that enable one to attain Buddhahood. All the Dharma doors are based on the foundation of the Three Conditions. It is like constructing a building. Regardless of its height and structural design, the building must have a firm foundation to be sound. TVKS

34. Although the Pure Land method allows one to bring one's residual karmas into the Western Pure Land, one must suppress one's sexual desire, anger, and ignorance. This way, one will be sure of attaining rebirth there. If one cannot suppress them, then no matter how much one chants the Buddha-name, it is as an ancient Chinese said: "Even if one chants until one's throat is hoarse, one's chanting is still futile." One will only form a good affinity with Amitabha

Buddha, but one will not succeed in attaining rebirth in the Pure Land in this lifetime. EILS

35. When our three karmas of body, speech, and mind are the same as Amitabha Buddha, we become his manifestation. We return to this world to fulfill his original vows. This is even more remarkable than being a person of virtue and sincerity. Originally, we are reborn in this world to repay our karmic debts, but now each of us is Amitabha Buddha coming to this world through the strength of our vows! This is the most remarkable and unsurpassable method in changing our destinies. CD

36. In the Western Pure Land, everyone has the same appearance, the same physical conditions, the same living environment, and the same learning. Everyone is equal in everything there. Therefore, one will not have afflictions such as arrogance or a sense of inferiority.

Although one still has the seeds of afflictions and residual habits, there are no conditions that will cause these afflictions and residual habits to arise. ASC

37. We should make a vow that when we attain rebirth in the Western Pure Land and attain Buddhahood, we will first help those beings we have killed.
"When I attain Buddhahood, you will be the first ones
I help. Please do not cause trouble or obstruct me. If
you obstruct me, I will not be able to succeed in cultivation, and you will continue to suffer in the Six
Paths."

The Dedication of Merit says ". . . repay the Four
Kinds of Kindness above, and relieve the suffering of
those in the Three Paths below." In the Three Paths,
the first ones to be helped are those who hold grudges
against us. EILS

38. When we encounter animals, we should mindfully
chant the Buddha-name and dedicate the merit to
them. It is quite usual to chant "Amituofo." It is even
better if we chant the Three Refuges. "Return and
rely upon the Buddha so as not to be reborn in the
hells. Return and rely upon the Dharma so as not to
be reborn as a hungry ghost. Return and rely upon
the Sangha so as not to reborn as an animal." We
chant this to the beings in the Three Evil Paths. When
we encounter animals, we can chant the Buddha-

name and dedicate the merit to them, as well as chant the Three Refuges. EILS

39. When we are reborn into the Pure Land through the state of Constant Mindfulness, we will be reborn in the Land Where Saints and Ordinary Beings Dwell Together. With the state of One Mind Undisturbed in Mindfulness, we will be reborn in the Land of Expedient Liberation. With the state of One Mind Undisturbed in Enlightenment, we will be reborn in the Land of True Reward. The level of attainment we achieve determines which land we will be reborn into.

There are also different levels in the state of Constant Mindfulness; thus, there are nine levels of birth. People who are reborn into the higher three levels of birth are able to pass away whenever they wish. At that time, they can go without any illness and may be standing or seated. If they do not feel like leaving this world yet, they can stay longer. Everything can be achieved at will.

People who are reborn into the middle three levels of birth are able to know a few months in advance when they are going to pass away. Again, they may leave this world standing or seated.

In the lower level, people will know several days in advance of their death, but they may become ill before their time of death. . . . In this lifetime we can attain the state of Constant Mindfulness in which we will have the ability to pass away at ease, to leave whenever we wish. This is to be reborn into the higher three levels of birth, into the Land Where Saints and Ordinary Beings Dwell Together, and to carry our remaining karma along with us. CD

40. Wandering thoughts are afflictions and karmic obstacles. As soon as they begin to rise, we will recognize them and change them into Amituofo. As the six senses encounter the external world and a wandering thought, which may be pleasurable or unpleasant, virtuous or unvirtuous arises, we immediately replace it with a second thought of either Amituofo or Namo Amituofo. Although the first thought is wandering and deluded, the second thought is Amituofo. This is to awaken. This awakening needs to be immediate so there is no room for delusion to grow. This is how we will effectively uncover our wisdom. CD

41. When one is often mindful of good dharmas, one's mind will be virtuous. When one often contemplates good dharmas, one's thoughts will be virtuous. When one often observes good dharmas, one's conduct will be virtuous. The criterion for virtuousness is to permanently end the Ten Evil Karmas: killing, stealing, committing sexual misconduct, lying, divisive speech, harsh speech, enticing speech, greed, anger, and ignorance. When one's every thought, every word, and every action accord with the Ten Virtuous Karmas and the virtues innate in the true nature, one will be free from all sufferings in the evil paths. BC

42. If we cannot attain Supreme, Perfect Enlightenment due to our insufficient efforts, it is all right as long as we can go to the Pure Land and meet Amitabha Buddha, for then we will uncover our true nature. This convenient and suitable method cannot be found in any other teaching. With others, if we do not achieve enlightenment, we will not be considered as having achieved attainment.

When we practice mindfulness of Amitabha Buddha, it is not necessary for us to be able to see the true nature. As long as we can see Amitabha Buddha, we will have achieved attainment. All our negative karma will be suppressed when we sincerely and single-mindedly chant. How can "Amituofo" have any negative karma? It is true and perfect goodness, not that of good or bad for such goodness is relative. True goodness has no duality and is the absolute great goodness. CD

Buddha-name Chanting

43. For a true practitioner who wants to have a fast, assured success in his practice in this lifetime, the Buddha-name is all he needs. One chants and reads the sutras to understand the truth. Once confidence is established upon one's understanding of the principles and the truth, one will naturally let go of everything else. Not only did Sakyamuni Buddha use this method as the foremost method to teach all beings, but all Buddhas do the same. The Pure Land method is hard to believe but easy to practice. Only when one has great good fortune and great wisdom will one be able to believe this method. EILS

44. The way to cultivate a pure mind is to mindfully chant the Buddha-name. When we are not chanting the Buddha-name, we should listen to the chanting of the Buddha-name. It is best if we can listen to our own chanting. So, we could record our chanting, and when we are not chanting, listen to this recording. This is very effective. This is cultivating a pure mind. EILS

45. As practitioners who chant the Buddha's name, if we are able to correct one fault daily and be mindful of Amitabha Buddha, then in three year's time we will be reborn into either the high or middle levels of the Pure Land. This is the way to cultivate to become a Buddha. The question is whether we are willing to do so earnestly. We are fooling ourselves if we are unable to find one fault daily. In failing to know them, we will fail to correct them. How can we hope to improve in this way? When there is no improvement, there is regression. To regard ourselves as infallible and that everything we do is correct is the most horrible way to live. CD

46. The Buddha-name chanting method is suitable for everyone to learn and practice regardless of one's capacity. Other methods such as Zen meditation and Tibetan Buddhism are not as easy for one to learn and practice. The Buddha-name chanting method is simple and convenient. It does not matter whether one has a Buddha image at home or if one has flowers to offer. Everyone can learn and practice. This method does not emphasize appearances or learning environment. It is the most convenient method. EILS

47. The Buddha said: "All dharmas are created by the mind." When we think about a matter [that will benefit others] every moment of every day, never forgetting it, then this matter will be successfully accomplished. If we think, "This is so difficult. I cannot do it. Forget it!" then this matter will not be accomplished. Why? Because when we stop thinking of benefitting others, we stop generating energy. Thoughts will truly generate inconceivable energy—this is continual mindfulness.

When one understands this principle, one sees that those who are mindful of Buddha will attain Buddhahood. A practitioner who chants the Buddha-name will definitely attain rebirth in the Western Pure Land—this is also the same principle. When one mindfully chants "Amituofo" and is mindful of the Western Pure Land—being diligently mindful without any interruption—Amitabha Buddha will definitely come to one. EILS

48. Purity of mind can suppress the negative karma accumulated over infinite past eons. How can we attain purity of mind, stillness of thought? We can do so through the unmoved mind that is in deep concentra-

tion. This is called One Mind Undisturbed in the method of chanting mindfully the Buddha's name. Once we attain this state, all of our negative karma will be suppressed. However, when a new wandering thought arises, our negative karma will again materialize. CD

49. If we want to practice filial piety to perfection, we just need to single-mindedly chant the Buddha-name and seek rebirth in the Western Pure Land. When we meet Amitabha Buddha, our filial piety will then be perfect. It is because [once we are in the Pure Land] we will be able to recognize our parents and also all our parents in past lifetimes and clearly know which paths they are in, so that when the conditions are mature, they will listen and accept our advice to mindfully chant the Buddha-name when we urge them to. This way, we will have the ability to help them. We will be able to help our families, friends, and those who have an affinity with us—from every one of our lifetimes—transcend the Six Paths, attain rebirth in the Western Pure Land, and attain Buddhahood. This is great filial piety! This is true filial piety! EILS

50. Single-mindedly chanting "Amituofo" day and night will reduce all of our wandering thoughts into one thought of Amituofo. Is Amituofo good or bad? Neither. It has nothing to do with the duality of good and bad for it accords with our true nature. The duality of good and bad only exists in our conscious minds, not in our true minds. With prolonged practice, we will naturally attain enlightenment if we are constantly mindful of Amituofo. Among eighty-four thousand methods, this method is unsurpassed. CD

51. The cultivation method that we practice is mindfully reciting the name of Amitabha Buddha. What is the meaning of Amitabha Buddha? Amitabha means infinite, and Buddha means wisdom and awakening. Therefore, Amitabha Buddha means infinite wisdom and infinite awakening. This is a good thought. Infinite wisdom and awakening is Buddha-nature. In the case of phenomena, it is Dharma-nature.

When we chant Amitabha Buddha, we are chanting Dharma-nature. Wisdom and awakening reside in everything in the universe. Wisdom and awakening are innate in everything in the universe. Wisdom and awakening pervade the whole universe. This Dharma door of mindfully reciting the Buddha-name is absolutely perfect. This is the state described in the *Avatamsaka Sutra*. ASC

52. Single-mindedly chanting "Amituofo" day and night will reduce all of our wandering thoughts into one thought of "Amituofo." Is "Amituofo" good or bad? Neither. It has nothing to do with the duality of good and bad for it accords with our true nature. The duality of good and bad only exists in our conscious minds, not in our true minds.

With prolonged practice, we will naturally attain enlightenment if we are constantly mindful of "Amituofo." Among eighty-four thousand methods, this method is unsurpassed. CD

53. Some people may say that when one chants mantras, one will also get help from Buddhas and bodhisattvas. Indeed, when chanting mantras as practiced by the Esoteric school, the Buddhas and bodhisattvas will also be there to help, but it is not as good as chanting the name of Amitabha Buddha. When one chants mantras, one will have the help of one or two Buddhas or bodhisattvas. To have the help of three to

five Buddhas and bodhisattvas is incredible. But when one mindfully chants the name of Amitabha Buddha, one will have the help of all the Buddhas in the ten directions and in the three time periods. This is why the merit of the name of Amitabha Buddha is inconceivable! EILS

54. What does proper thought arising mean? It is "Amituofo": the most truthful and ultimate proper thought. The only important issue in our life is to constantly maintain proper thoughts, to not cling to deviated or erroneous ones, and to be constantly mindful of Amitabha Buddha day and night, without interruption. If we can continue our cultivation in this way, then in three months we will receive wonderful results. If we can constantly maintain mindfulness of Amitabha Buddha, with this one thought we are assured of reducing our wandering discriminatory thoughts.

It is impossible for us to not have any wandering thoughts. Do not be afraid of them so long as thoughts of Amitabha Buddha can occupy us the most: such as sixty percent of our thoughts of Amitabha Buddha with only forty percent that are wandering. If we are not constantly mindful of Amitabha Buddha, then our minds will be filled with wandering thoughts.

If we can continue this practice for three months, increasing the thoughts of Amitabha Buddha and decreasing our wandering thoughts, we will be at ease and free in spirit. Our minds will become more serene and our joy from practicing the teachings will show that our karmic obstacles have been reduced. In the past, our minds were filled with afflictions and worries, and our futures looked dark. Now we can be happy, confident, and wise as our lives become interesting, and our futures become bright. CD

55. At all times, when one single-mindedly chants the Buddha-name, the mind will be free of all wandering thoughts, afflictions, worries, and concerns. Mindfully chanting the Buddha-name will thus tame all of one's faculties. One's body will be supple and one's mind will be gentle. One will be able to achieve physical and mental well-being. EILS

56. We may want to ask, "What is the method that the bodhisattvas of the Western Pure Land practice to

achieve taming all their faculties and having a supple body and gentle mind?" It is mindfully chanting "Amituofo."

As Mahasthamaprapta Bodhisattva said, "I and fifty-two fellow practitioners . . . ." "Fifty-two" refers to the ten stages of faith, ten stages of abiding, ten stages of practice, ten stages of dedication, ten stages of ground, the stage of equal enlightenment, and the stage of wondrous enlightenment. "Fellow practitioners" refers to practitioners who shared the same aspiration and focused on practicing the Pure Land method. This tells us that from Mahasthamaprapta Bodhisattva's initial generation of the bodhi mind until attainment of Buddhahood, he practiced the chanting of "Amituofo," without any changes. This is truly inconceivable! Chanting "Amituofo" enables us ordinary beings to attain Buddhahood. EILS

57. To practice good deeds with one sincere mind means to have an absolute proper and virtuous thought as the first thought. There are no wandering second thoughts. To chant "Amituofo," is to single-mindedly practice Constant Mindfulness of Amitabha Buddha and wholeheartedly seek rebirth into the

Pure Land. The most marvelous way to reform and reduce our karmic obstacles is to have no wandering thoughts. This does not mean to not have any proper thoughts. Without proper thoughts, we become ignorant. Wandering thoughts are discriminatory thoughts and attachments. It is not easy for average people to achieve the state of no wandering thought. But everyone can achieve this by practicing the Buddha Mindfulness Chanting method. CD

58. This is an unsurpassed principle. Purity of mind can suppress the negative karma accumulated over infinite past eons. How can we attain purity of mind, stillness of thought? We can do so through the unmoved mind that is in deep concentration. This is called "One Mind Undisturbed" in the method of chanting mindfully the Buddha's name. Once we attain this state, all of our negative karma will be suppressed. However, when a new wandering thought arises, our negative karma will again materialize. CD

59. By single-mindedly chanting the Buddha-name, we will taste boundless meanings and flavor. After we taste the flavor of the Dharma, there will be no stop-

ping us. During our learning, we will truly feel joy and will definitely be making courageous and diligent progress.

Now, when we chant the Buddha-name we do not taste any flavor of the Dharma because when we chant "Amituofo" we are thinking of other things. This is the reason that our cultivation has not gone anywhere. We should diligently continue with our chanting. Anything that obstructs us from single-mindedly chanting should be discarded.

In addition, we should chant with a sincere, pure, and respectful mind. After chanting in this way for half a year, we will taste the flavor of the Dharma. When we do, we will have confidence in attaining rebirth in the Western Pure Land. The more we chant, the firmer our confidence. We will be able to know in advance the time of our rebirth. EILS

60. How does one subdue and transform one's thoughts? When an evil thought arises, one should instantly have the wisdom to be aware of it and stop the wandering thought. For many kalpas, for which there is no beginning, ordinary beings have been immersed in affliction and habits, so they naturally have

many wandering thoughts. But as it is said, "Do not fear a thought arising; fear realizing it too late." When an evil thought arises, one should immediately detect it and transform it into "Amituofo." This is cultivation. In the Zen school, this is the practice of enlightening illumination. Here is where we practice: transforming an evil thought into a virtuous thought, transforming an evil thought into "Amituofo." The thought of "Amituofo" is the most virtuous. There is no thought more virtuous than this. EILS

61. The "Chapter on the Perfect and Complete Realization of Mahasthamaprapta" from the *Surangama Sutra* tells us how Mahasthamaprapta Bodhisattva concentrated on Buddha-name Recitation from the time he took refuge until the time he attained enlightenment. He taught us that the proper way to chant is the complementary practice of concentrating the six sense organs and continuous pure mindfulness of Amitabha Buddha. Pure mindfulness is to chant with a pure mind and without doubt or any intermingling with other thoughts or methods. Continuous is the uninterrupted chanting with one word after another and is the key to success in the practice of Buddha-

name Recitation that was taught by Mahasthama-prapta Bodhisattva. BACW

Sutra Recitation

62. Single-mindedly chanting a sutra without wandering thoughts, distractions, or doubt—this is cultivating meditative concentration. From start to finish, enunciating clearly every word without mistake or omission—this is cultivating wisdom: fundamental wisdom. Thus, chanting a sutra is cultivating simultaneously the precepts, meditative concentration, and wisdom. If one thinks about the meaning of the sutra while chanting it, it will ruin the cultivation of precept observation, meditative concentration, and wisdom [the Three Learnings]. This is treating the sutra as a worldly book. EILS

63. My teacher Living Buddha Zhangjia said: "Buddhism does not emphasize forms or rituals, but rather true substance." If we pay attention only to the formality and fail to profoundly comprehend the essence of the sutra's teaching, we will not progress any further than just being zealous about our faith and thus be easily manipulated by those with bad intentions. REN

64. Chanting the sutras is cultivating the precepts, cultivating meditative concentration, and cultivating wisdom. When chanting a sutra one simply reads the words, without thinking of their meaning. Chanting sincerely this way is cultivating the precepts, meditative concentration, and wisdom.

The sutras are to be recited daily but not for the benefit of the Buddha. We recite them as another reminder of how to cultivate our mind and how to properly interact with others and circumstances. For example, our daily conduct is an expression of the *Infinite Life Sutra* when we emulate the qualities found within it. EILS

65. Sutras flow from the pure and quiet mind of the Buddha. When we develop a mind as pure and quiet, we will understand all we read in a sutra. The reason why a sutra is so hard to understand now is that our minds are filled with wandering thoughts. How can this mind be in harmony with one that is pure and quiet? This is why we do not understand the Buddha's words. So, if we want to learn from a good teacher, we need to trust and believe that their methods are proper and correct. BACW

66. The sutras help us to understand the true reality of life and the universe so that we will know the proper way to think and behave as well as the appropriate cultivation method to use. Only when we truly accord with the teachings of the sutra, will we benefit. BACW

67. If we chant or read indifferently without applying the principles, then all our efforts will be futile. Only when we become aware of the purpose and method of chanting the sutra can we actually achieve any results. . . . Today, people simply recite absentmindedly, like small children who sing a song with the right words to the right tune, but without understanding the meaning. Only when we become aware of the purpose and method of chanting the sutra can we actually achieve any results. BACW

68. If the Buddha's teachings are not integrated into our minds, and our minds are still dictated by our afflictions and habits, what is the use of chanting the sutras? Only our verbal karma is good; whereas our minds and behavior still remain unimproved. So while our chanting does plant a seed in our Alaya consciousness, the seed is dormant for now. But even

though the benefit is small and not immediate, it is better to chant a sutra than not to chant at all.

Whether you chant with a focused mind or with a wandering mind, you will plant a seed in your Alaya consciousness. If you chant with a focused mind and with sincerity, the vitality of the seed will be strong. If you chant with a wandering mind or with reluctance, the vitality of the seed will be weak. ASC

69. What is the first step in our learning Buddhism? Start by reciting one sutra. Do we need to understand it? No. For when we have not ended afflictions, our understanding will be erroneous. Then why do we recite only this sutra? By reciting the sutra, the Three Learnings of self-discipline, deep concentration and wisdom are accomplished together. BACW

70. Mr. Li Bingnan always told his students that when they listened to lectures, they needed to concentrate on understanding the principles in the sutra and not the words themselves. These principles are the laws governing the Buddha's teachings as well as worldly teachings. One, who thoroughly understands the principles of one sutra, can then use them to master all

sutras. To benefit, the student must conscientiously and wholeheartedly follow the methods taught by the teacher without being distracted by anything new or different. BACW

Principles

71. The teachings of Mahayana Buddhism emphasize perfect harmony, perfect wisdom, perfect undertakings, and perfect merits. People today should try to appreciate this point and learn from the teachings. Only the sages' teaching of wisdom can help us improve ourselves. Buddhism teaches us to eliminate our afflictions and bad habits. In other words, we are to correct our wrong thoughts, wrong mindsets, wandering thoughts, discrimination, and attachments, and accord with the rules of nature and the order in which nature functions.

We should understand the relationship between the entire universe and the rules of nature: the ultimate truth is that everything is indeed one entity and is harmonious. We and the universe and are one entity. LS

72. The reason why our merits cannot compare with those of Buddhas and bodhisattvas is the differences in the minds, in the intentions. The environment changes according to the mind. As ordinary people, we are very narrow-minded; thus, no matter how

much good fortune or how many merits we cultivate, we are bound by our discriminations and attachments. But these no longer bind bodhisattvas and arhats. Even when they perform a small deed, their merits are infinite. In understanding this principle, our every thought will be perfect, and our merits and virtues will be infinite. CD

73. Why does conflict arise? Because one's thoughts, speech, and behavior do not accord with the innate virtuousness of one's nature. When one's thoughts and behavior do not accord with one's nature, conflict will arise. Why can't one's thoughts and behavior accord with one's nature? If we look carefully, we will find that the origin of conflict is greed. Therefore, in the teaching of Sakyamuni, greed, anger, and ignorance are considered the root causes of conflict and are called the Three Poisons. The most fundamental among the Three Poisons is greed—one's greed for material gain. LS

74. We see that the universe is ever changing, and the changing never stops for a second. Buddhism calls this "instantaneous arising and ceasing." When the

tide rises, it is "arising"; when the tide ebbs, it is "ceasing." We usually see only the constantly changing phenomena, but we do not see the noumenon that manifests these changing phenomena.

Although all phenomena arise and cease instantaneously, and are constantly changing, the noumenon of the universe that manifests and makes changes possible does not change at all. It has the qualities of neither arising nor ceasing, neither coming nor going, neither eternal nor impermanent, and neither one nor many. These are the qualities used to describe the noumenon of the universe. It is our "original face before birth." ASC

75. Needless worrying is also an indication of karmic obstacles. The past is past, what is the use of dwelling on it? Tomorrow is yet to come. To wonder about it is to have wandering thoughts. Some people are extremely good at worrying and wondering about the past and the future. They can do so all day long. This is to make a mountain out of a molehill and this is a karmic obstacle. CD

76. What kind of mind are we using now? The deluded mind, not the true mind. There is no hindrance in the true mind. With the deluded mind, when we try to see something with our naked eyes, we cannot see it clearly.

It is like looking through distorted glasses, seeing the external environment through a layer of delusion. This delusion is the Eight Consciousnesses and fifty-one mind objects. With the glasses heavily contaminated, we then interact with the external environment through these consciousnesses and mind objects. Therefore, the environment has changed to that of the Six Dusts.

When these consciousnesses and mind objects are not applied to see the external environment, then we do not see the environment of the Six Dusts but that of the true nature. CD

77. Our every thought and every action are recorded, like the data in a computer. Our Alaya Consciousness records all our good and evil thoughts and actions, similar to what a computer does. This is our database, containing not only data in this lifetime but also data from all past lifetimes. Spiritual beings and people

who have the ability can read our data. Therefore, we should be cautious with our thoughts. We should not allow any evil thought to arise. Every thought should be of benefiting all beings and not be of harming them. This way, we will truly succeed in attaining great virtue. EILS

78. Greed, anger, ignorance, arrogance and doubt are the roots of all natural disasters. They are also the root causes of human diseases. When one has the causes of illness—greed, anger, ignorance, arrogance and doubt—in one's mind, one tends to feel resentment, hatred, vexation, anger, and annoyance and thus gives rise to thoughts of killing, stealing, sexual misconduct, and lying. The retributions will be the malfunction of the internal organs and the occurrence of diseases and epidemics. SC

79. When I wanted to study Buddhism with Mr. Li Bingnan and to formally become his student, he put forward three conditions: "First, from today on, you can only listen to my lectures. You are not allowed to listen to any other Dharma masters or lay practitioners. Second, from today on, you are not allowed to

read any book, be it a sutra or any kind of book, without my permission." The first condition blocked my ears, and the second covered my eyes. "Third, what you have learned does not count with me. You are to forget it all. Today, you start anew with me."

These three conditions were very harsh. When I first heard them, I thought that this teacher was very autocratic, domineering, and unreasonable. He sounded so incredibly arrogant. Nevertheless, after consideration, I accepted his conditions and became his student. I did not know then that these conditions were precepts meant to help me cut off my afflictions.

The more one sees and listens, the more afflictions one has; the less one sees and listens or when one does not see or listen, one will have no afflictions. So, my teacher used this method to help me fulfill the vow of "Afflictions are inexhaustible; I vow to end them all." BACW2

80. When we, as ordinary people, look around us, we see only the illusory, ever-changing phenomena, not the truth of these phenomena. It is like looking at a stormy sea. We tend to see waves and surf. We forget

the truth. What is the truth? The truth is that the waves and surf are water. ASC

81. When the Buddha said that all phenomena are empty, he meant that the noumenon is empty: all the phenomena do not have self-nature and are empty in themselves. Everything is empty and without self. "Self" implies being in control. "Everything is empty and without self" means that no one controls the phenomena.

Then, how do phenomena come about? They arise from the combination of various conditions. Boundless conditions gather and generate them. Therefore, phenomena do not have self-nature or self-identity.

When we are clear about this truth, we should absolutely not attach to any phenomena or give rise to any thought. The mind should always be pure, impartial, and awakened. EILS

82. If we see someone in need and unreservedly give him one dollar, then the merit of this accords with our true nature because at that time we did not discriminate between others and us. We did not distinguish between receiver and donor. We were not attached. In

this way, the merits from giving one dollar are infinite for they are the uncovering of our virtuous natures. CD

83. Jealousy and hatred are indeed thoughts of stealing. Why? Because one does not like to see others doing better. This mindset is not normal. Wishing that others be worse off, or becoming displeased, critical or slanderous when seeing virtuous people or good deeds being done—these are all thoughts of stealing.

A virtuous person delights upon seeing other virtuous people or good deeds and will wholeheartedly assist these people and help them accomplish their good deeds. A virtuous person will set a good example for whatever community he is in, and his good deeds will definitely benefit the general public.

When we help others achieve their goals, we will succeed in our cultivation of virtues. When we obstruct others, we are committing tremendously grave offenses. EILS

84. If our every thought is of self-benefit, our self-attachment will grow daily. Even as we plant some good causes, our attachments will increase. The Bud-

dha told us that if we wished to transcend the cycle of birth and death, we must rid ourselves of both self and knowledge-attachment. Self-attachments are afflictions that hinder us from attaining purity of mind. Knowledge-attachment hinders us from uncovering our all-knowing wisdom, our true wisdom. BACW

85. What exactly is no wandering thoughts? What is correct thought? Having no wandering thoughts is being free of all wandering thoughts, all discriminations, and all attachments. Correct thought is a clear and correct understanding of all principles and matters, causes and results, and the noumenon of anything and its phenomenal expressions. Therefore, in correct thought, there is wisdom, and there are virtues and capabilities, and auspicious marks. In correct thought, there are no wandering thoughts, discriminations, and attachments. ASC

86. The *Diamond Sutra* says: "Even the Dharma has to be laid aside, let alone worldly teachings." "Dharma" refers to the Buddhadharma. One should not be attached to the Buddhadharma either. Any attachment is a mistake.

The Buddhadharma is like a boat, something we use for crossing a river. Upon reaching our destination, we should let go of the tool that got us there. The Buddhadharma is to help us overcome difficulties. When we have done so, we should not be attached to the Buddhadharma and should let go of it too. EILS

87. As ordinary beings with far too many wanderings thoughts, discriminations, and attachments, we view everything dualistically. We do not view all phenomena as one. When our true wisdom manifests, we will know that all phenomena are one, not two.

Take the lid of a mug for example. It is concave on one side but it is convex on the other side. If people do not understand this truth, then two people standing on different sides of the lid will quarrel over whether the lid is concave or convex. This is because they look at the lid from different sides. When they see both sides of the lid, they will realize that concave is no different from convex. They are one, not two. ASC

88. Ancient sages said that a wise and virtuous person knows that everything including "one sip and one

bite" is destined. However, foolish people relentlessly pursue things that are already destined to be theirs. CD

89. There is no need to be overly serious or to criticize everything. As we have learned in the *Diamond Sutra*: "All phenomena are illusory, like dreams, mirages, bubbles, shadows." Nothing is real. As the ancients said, all phenomena are as fleeting as clouds. There is nothing worthy of anger or dispute. There is no point in dwelling on things, for this will hinder our cultivation of purity of mind. CD

90. In Great Master Ouyi's commentary on the *Amitabha Sutra*, we read, "One lets go of the phenomena one sees and keeps in mind and never reminisces about them." Letting go refers to how we are to react to our external environments.

Outside stimuli often tempt us. But, ideally, when we see or hear these stimuli, we should not be attached to them. When they are over, we should not reminisce about them again. Every time we recall them, a seed is planted in our Alaya consciousness, and we create a karmic cause. Our mouths are not creating a karmic cause, neither are our bodies. It is our thoughts that are creating karmic cause. ASC

91. Mahayana bodhisattvas cherish the heart to help all sentient beings. They not only know their own suffering and try to help themselves, but they also want to help all sentient beings. To equally wish to help all beings is the great bodhi mind. The *Infinite Life Sutra* tells us that bodhisattvas "befriend and voluntarily help all living beings." Even if we do not request it, they come to help. To voluntarily introduce Buddhism to all is the pure cause of a bodhisattva.

To help all beings, we first need to know how to help ourselves. To do this we free ourselves from worries and afflictions. BACW

92. All of our encounters in life, whether good fortune or bad fortune, good luck or bad luck, wealth or poverty—all are destined. Ordinary people cannot change this. If we are not supposed to have something, no amount of trying to hold on to it will succeed for long. Conversely, we will naturally receive what we are supposed to. It is not worth the effort to do what is

wrong and to risk all in the hope of attaining self-satisfaction. CD

93. Conditions may be favorable or adverse. When an adverse condition appears, one should know that it results from a bad cause planted in the past. If a person displeases one or goes against one, then one should just laugh it off, as this will cancel out the karmic debt incurred in the past. If one becomes angry, one will incur another debt on top of the old debt. Instead of canceling out the old debt, one will have even more problems. As it is said, "If one owes money, one will repay with money. If one owes life, one will repay with life. Reprisal breeds reprisal. It is cyclical and never ending." EILS

94. This principle, "to cultivate one is to cultivate all" was explained in the *Avatamsaka Sutra*. It is the learning and cultivation of non-hindrance. Everything arises from our true nature. If the cultivation is in accordance with the true nature, then it can be regarded as cultivating all. If we do good deeds that are not from our true nature and because we are seeking, we will only receive what we seek—nothing more. If we

seek from the true nature, then not only will we attain what we seek, but also we will gain infinite benefits. CD

95. Many practitioners have voiced the concern over what they should do because they found it hard to maintain their aspiration for enlightenment and they often retrogressed. These practitioners stated the truth. It is indeed very easy to retrogress. It is up to oneself to think of a way to prevent oneself from retrogressing. Because people have different capacities and karmas, there is no one fixed method. If there were a specific method suitable for everyone despite their different capacities, then Sakyamuni Buddha would not have needed to teach eighty-four Dharma doors, or countless Dharma doors. He would only have needed to teach one Dharma door! ASC

96. Greed is the cause of the karma that results in us being born into the hungry ghost realm. By failing to rid ourselves of the resentment and anger caused by greed, we will be born into the hell realm. Ignorance, having no wisdom, results in us being born in the animal realm.

In both worldly teachings and in Buddhism there is truth and falsehood, justice and injustice, right and wrong, good and bad. An ignorant person cannot tell the difference between them. Intentional or unintentional, he or she often confuses falsehood and truth, bad and good. BACW

97. When we observe all the worries, pain, bitterness, anger, good fortune, misfortune, good, evil, conflicts, confrontations, and natural disasters around the world, we see that they are due to the wrong understanding of the truth about life and the universe.

From this misunderstanding, we erroneously generate emotional attachments, differentiate between others and ourselves, and expand the conflicts and confrontations within ourselves to all beings, affairs, objects, and the natural environment outside ourselves. This is why we have worsening disasters everywhere.

In reality, natural disasters are caused by human minds. The Buddha said: "Greed is the cause of flood. Anger is the cause of fire. Ignorance is the cause of wind. Arrogance and inequality are the cause of earthquakes." REN

98. Once we understand the fundamental principles, we will understand that everything in this world and beyond arises from the mind and changes according to our perceptions. If we seek to become Buddhas, we will become Buddhas. If we seek to become heavenly beings, we will become heavenly beings. Everything accords with the mind. The *Avatamsaka Sutra* tells us: "We should observe the nature of the Dharma Realm as everything is created by the mind." Therefore, the way of seeking is to accord with the principle that everything arises from the mind and is changed by our perceptions. CD

99. The practice of patience and tolerance is extremely important. Only when we are capable of enduring everything, can our hearts can be pure and unaffected by external influences. When we can be unaffected, our external environment will better accord with our thoughts. WPH

100. We often hear about renunciation in Buddhism. For the vast majority of Buddhists, renunciation does not mean giving up a worldly life and becoming a monastic. It means letting go of one's attachments. The

Buddha showed us how for he had no attachments to this world. Unfortunately, as ordinary beings we are still very much attached to the world in our every thought. Although the Mahayana teachings emphasize substance rather than form, if there is substance, it will certainly be reflected in form. Therefore, if our thoughts transcend this world, our behavior will reflect this. ASC

101. It is erroneous to [have thoughts of] not wishing for something, because one would reject all opportunities. [Thoughts of] wishing for something is seeking affinities. [Thoughts of] not wishing for something is also seeking affinities. Therefore, bodhisattvas practice the Middle Way: when they teach beings, they are according with conditions, not seeking affinities. EILS

102. We often read in the sutras of the fire burning our forest of merits. What is this fire? It is anger and hatred. When we lose our tempers, we lose our merits as well. If you want to know how much merit you have, think of the last time you became angry. With one angry thought, the fire burns our forest of merits.

What is merit? It is purity of mind, concentration, and wisdom. Think about it, if we lose our tempers, how can we maintain our concentration and wisdom? Impossible. As for good fortune, it is our wealth and intelligence. When our mind attains Constant Mindfulness of Buddha Amitabha or One Mind Undisturbed, we can accumulate merits and virtues. But with just one outburst of temper, all is lost: no more Constant Mindfulness of Buddha Amitabha, much less One Mind Undisturbed. Therefore, we need to remain vigilant so as not to lose our merits. CD

103. The Buddha told us that if we practice the Ten Virtuous Karmas, we will not fall into the Three Bad Realms. Instead, we would likely to be born in the heaven realms if we practice these good conducts diligently. If we achieve the deep concentration along with the Four Immeasurable Minds of loving-kindness (giving happiness to others), compassion (taking away bitterness of others), joy (liberating others from suffering and feeling happy for them) and letting go (of the first three minds), we will rise to an even higher level of the heavens, the Heaven of Form and the Heaven of Formless. BACW

104. The law of causality never changes, either in this world or beyond; the more wealth we give, the more wealth we will gain. We do not even know where this wealth will come from, but it will come. The more teaching we give, the more wisdom we will gain, so we do not want to withhold any of our wealth or knowledge. Poverty is the result of not giving wealth. Ignorance is the result of not giving teaching, and illness and short lives are the result of not giving fearlessness. CD

105. If we seek to resolve disasters and conflicts, we must start from within our own body and mind. We need to truly affirm that all beings are one. All phenomenon are in harmony originally. Thinking thus, we will naturally be sincere, compassionate, peaceful, respectful, humble, and loving.

In the *Infinite Life Sutra*, it is stated: "Wherever the Buddha's teachings flourish, either in cities or countrysides, people will gain inconceivable benefits. The land and people will be enveloped in peace. The sun and moon will shine clear and bright. Wind and rain will appear accordingly and there will be no disasters. Nations will be prosperous and there will be no need for soldiers or weapons. People will abide by morality and accord with laws. They will be courteous and humble, and everyone will be content, without injustices. There will be no thefts or violence. The strong will not dominate the weak and everyone will get their fair share." REN

106. Today, many people are seriously ill. Why do they become ill? Where do the illnesses come from? The root cause is our anger. If we can calm down and never get angry, there will be no more illness. When we learn that, we will be healthy. Although there are still many people and reasons out there that can make us angry, (we Buddhists call them our karmic creditors), we do not have to be so obedient and get angry when they irritate us. If we get angry once they irritate us, then we are fooled.

We have to know the truth. They are here to make me angry. I know that, and I will not follow their will. On the contrary, I will smile at them. In this way, no one can harm me.

Who can harm us? Actually, we can only be harmed by ourselves! If we can learn this, no matter how hard people try to irritate us, we will be impervious. If we can be impervious, we will truly see through to the truth and let go of everything. WPH

107. When bad causes created in the past encounter present adverse conditions, the retributions for these wrongdoings mature. However, if we refrain from committing further misdeeds, we can suppress the adverse conditions. The bad causes still exist, but without the right conditions, they will not mature. The principle in changing destiny is based on this conditional aspect of the law of causality. Cause is what was created in the past and is unchangeable; but condition is changeable and controllable.

We reap what we sow. We can plant melon and bean seeds—these are causes. When we do so, we will grow melons and beans—these are the fruits, the results. But we cannot grow beans from melon seeds or melons from bean seeds. Cause is a constant here. What we will harvest depends on the conditions. If we would like to harvest beans, we plant the seeds for them and put away the melon seeds.

For a cause to come into effect, appropriate conditions are required. For example, seeds need the right conditions, which are good soil, fertilizer, sun, and

water to grow well. Even after the seeds are planted—and a cause thus created—we can prevent them
from maturing. We simply withhold the water and
sunlight. The seeds will not grow. They will not mature into fruits because they do not have the right
conditions. CD

108. In Buddhism, we are taught not only to love, but
that our love also needs to arise from a mind of sincerity, purity, and equality. We call this kind of love
compassion. Compassion is rational love. We also
need to use true wisdom. Wisdom is the true mind
and emotion is the illusory mind. Love that arises
from emotions will change while love that arises from
wisdom will never change. Hence, Buddhas do not
use love, but instead use compassion.

On appearance, love and compassion seem the
same, but their intentions are different. Love may
change to hatred but with wisdom, love will never
change. All Buddhas and bodhisattvas will love us no
matter what; whether we love or hate them, become
jealous, or slander, harm or destroy them. Their compassion for us will never change. This is true love.
TVKS

109. Most of us will find that our six senses become polluted when they encounter external surroundings. When these are pleasing, we develop a heart of greed—this is pollution. When these are displeasing, we develop a heart of resentment and anger, which is pollution as well.

We need to remember that the Five Desires of wealth, sex, fame, food, and sleep and the Seven Human Emotions of joy, anger, sorrow, fear, love, hate, and desire are impurities of the heart. Originally, our true nature was pure without impurities. We need to eradicate all impurities and rely upon our pure heart. BACW

110. The sutras tell us: "Cause and effect are linked through the past, present and future." What we undergo in this lifetime are the consequences of what we had done in our previous lifetimes, while what we do now will determine what we undergo in our future lifetimes. If we cultivate very diligently, we need not wait until future lifetimes to reap our rewards; instead, we may see our deeds bear fruit in this lifetime! CD

111. We should be impartial to all people in any situation, whether they are good or bad. An impartial mind will lead to a pure mind. Attachment as well as dissatisfaction and enmity are wandering thoughts. When one is free of all wandering thoughts, all discriminations, and all attachments, one will attain a pure and impartial mind. When the mind is pure and impartial, one will definitely be awakened, not deluded. One will then realize the goal of "purity, impartiality, and enlightenment." EILS

112. We read in the Mahayana sutras: "All phenomena are manifested by the mind" and "Our environment changes according to our mind." "Environment" here means mountains, rivers, earth, trees, flowers, and grass. They can all be changed by our minds. We have to remember this sentence.

If I can be a person with a pure, virtuous, sincere, compassionate mind, then the mountains, rivers, earth, trees, flowers, and grass will become strong and wonderful. If my mind is full of greed, anger, ignorance, and arrogance, and my thoughts are constantly of taking advantage of others to benefit myself, then the outer world will become fragile. WPH

113. The true nature is of the utmost purity and virtuousness. It is perfect and radiant. Habits are the bad thoughts and views that one acquired after birth. Simply put, the conflict between the true nature and acquired habits is the conflict between altruism and self-benefit. Compassion, loving-kindness, and all virtues are innate in the true nature of all beings; selfishness and all bad thoughts are not. OH

114. The Buddha taught us that wealth, wisdom, and long life are all karmic results. If we want to obtain the result, we must first establish and nurture the cause. Good causes bring about good results: bad causes garner bad results. Where there is a cause, there will be a result and where there is a result, there was a cause. This is a natural law that never changes and the law around which all other laws in the universe revolve.

Where do disasters come from? They are the manifestations of our minds. They occur because our minds are impure, with too many aberrant thoughts, which is why we have so many disasters on our planet. The *Surangama Sutra* tells us clearly that our consuming greed can result in floods. Our consuming anger can result in fire, causing volcanic eruptions and escalating the temperature of our planet. When our planet gets angry, she shows her temper through volcanic eruptions. Ignorance brings about disasters caused by typhoons and hurricanes. Arrogance results in earthquakes. When we are arrogant, our mind is no longer just and we lose our sense of equality. Inequality in our mind causes earthquakes.

Therefore, greed, anger, ignorance, and arrogance are the four root causes of the four different disasters. WPH

115. Whether attaining something outside of ourselves such as material objects or inside ourselves such as virtues, we still need to seek from within, from the mind. Seeking from the outside would be futile. Why? The outside factor is a constant—it cannot change. The mind is a variable—it changes.   CD

116. How do man-made calamities, war, for example, come about? They are from the confrontational and conflicting thoughts in our minds. For example, when there is profit, who do we think of benefitting first? If we think of ourselves first, then it will be difficult to

avoid conflicts of interest with others. If everyone thinks of him- or herself, how can this world be safe and secure?

On the other hand, if everyone can put others before themselves, how can this world be in disorder? WPH

117. Many scientists now believe that everything in this world is composed of elementary particles such as electrons and quarks, and that they are all actually tiny quantum particles (photons) vibrating at different frequencies. Those quanta that vibrate very slowly form rocks and minerals. Those vibrating faster form animals, plants, and human beings. Those vibrating even faster become television and radio signals. Everything in this universe is made up of quanta that are generated intensively and continuously, and these quanta originate and die at a speed faster than we can imagine. MR

118. If one has the slightest thought of self, trouble will follow. Why? Because one makes mistakes when one has even a thought of self-interest. Only when one has no thought of self-interest and has truly let go

of everything will one's mind be liberated and one's wisdom be uncovered. ASC

119. To reconcile conflict, it is imperative to decrease and eventually let go of the desire for material gain. The opposite of material gain is benevolence and justice, which is compassion (*cibei*) as taught in Buddhism. Benevolence is ci—helping all beings attain happiness and sacrificing oneself for others. Justice refers to helping all beings end suffering. It is equivalent to bei. Therefore, Buddhism advocates "Compassion is the essence, and expediency is the means," while Confucianism teaches benevolence and justice. Although the words used are different, they convey the same meaning. Mencius' method of solving a problem is exactly the same as that of the Buddha: they both start from the root causes. LS

120. Matter is accumulated from units of consciousness, (the rapid arising and ceasing of thoughts). There is no matter that exists without consciousness. Both physical and mental phenomena are derived from our thoughts. Once our thought arises, various phenomena in the universe appear. Once our thought

ceases, the universe disappears and at the same time our true nature instantly emerges. SE

121. All phenomena in the universe are one entity and are the manifestation of the true nature. When one thought arises, all objects instantly appear. When there is one existence, all exist. When one existence ceases, all existence ceases. There is no order or before and after. It is much like the television screen that changes images all the time, but all the changes come from one screen. Different images are the result of different frequencies of transmission. The change of frequency can be compared to the change of thoughts. When one thought arises, all objects follows. That is why Buddha said: "All phenomenon arises from the mind." REN

122. We need to avoid all that is evil and embrace all that is good. We begin with ourselves. First, we cannot allow ourselves to be affected by worldly phenomena. In other words, we must not be attached to the Five Desires and the Six Sense Objects but let go of them, for as long as we cling to them, we will never eradicate our selfishness. These thoughts of self-

benefit are the root of all negative karma. All good deeds that are done out of evil intentions will become evil. CD

123. A person who has a thorough and correct understanding of the truth of life and the universe—all principles and matters, the noumenon of anything and its phenomenal expressions, and causes and results—is called a Buddha. A sage also has a clear understanding of the truth of life and the universe but not thoroughly. The difference between a Buddha and a sage is the extent of understanding. AL

124. Confucianism and Buddhism both teach us to be better people, to be virtuous, and to achieve universal harmony after we achieve personal harmony. The Buddha said in the *Ten Virtuous Karmas Sutra* that bodhisattvas have a method that can help them end all sufferings in the Three Evil Paths. The method is being mindful of and contemplating wholesome thoughts often, and observing wholesome behavior and speech night and day, without having even the slightest non-virtuous thought. This way, one will end all evils for-

ever and perfectly accomplish good dharmas—wholesome thoughts, behavior and speech. BC

125. When we contemplate carefully, we see that all the complex problems throughout history and around the world arise from contradiction, conflict, opposition, and inequality. When we probe deeper, we see that the root of conflict is the conflict between the true nature and the acquired habits of humanity. In other words, it is the conflict between altruism and self-benefit.

Therefore, the Buddha taught this fundamental principle: "When the mind is pure, the land will be pure. When the mind is at peace, all beings will be at peace. When the mind is impartial, the world will enjoy equality." He taught us to purify ourselves, enrich our spiritual life, return to our original goodness, and achieve harmony of body and mind. This way, all the contradictions, conflicts, oppositions, and inequalities in the world will naturally be resolved. BC

126. If our every thought is of ourselves, ego-attachment will worsen day by day. How then can we transcend the Three Realms? This is why the Buddha

taught us to always think of benefiting all beings. This way, the thoughts of benefiting ourselves will gradually diminish and go away. Our every thought and every deed should be for all beings, not for ourselves.

When all beings have good fortune, we too have good fortune, because we are also one of the beings. Similarly, we cannot avoid misfortune if all beings have misfortune. EILS

127. Goodness springing from our hearts arises from true sincerity and is true goodness. What is true goodness and false goodness? We must look into our hearts to see if we are genuinely practicing goodness. False goodness is simply following others, to act without sincerity while wishing for a return. True goodness is to wish for nothing in return. CD

128. Learning and practicing Buddhism is nothing other than letting go of wandering thoughts, discriminations, and attachments. When one does so, the true mind will manifest. It is true that "in Buddhism, every wish can be fulfilled." EILS

129. We often read in the sutras of the fire burning our forest of merits. What is this fire? It is anger and hatred. When we lose our tempers, we lose our merits as well. If you want to know how much merit you have, think of the last time you became angry. With one angry thought, the fire burns our forest of merits.

Why do all our merits get destroyed with just a little anger? Because we lose our purity of mind. Therefore, all the teachings and attainments are based on patience and deep concentration. They are not only the key to our cultivation in transcending the cycle of rebirth, but the key to worldly matters as well. "To remain unmoved by slander" is deep concentration and is the revelation of wisdom. To become angry due to slander is a manifestation of karmic obstacles. We can choose whether to have our wisdom revealed or our karmic obstacles materialize. CD

130. If one seeks wisdom, one must achieve a pure mind. When one has a pure mind, wisdom manifests. A pure mind is like a mirror. Its function is to see everything clearly in its reflection. This [seeing everything clearly] is having wisdom. If one wants to have a pure mind, one's mind must not be contaminated

even in the slightest way—by mundane teachings (the Five Desires and the Six Dusts) or by supramundane teachings (that is, Mahayana, Theravada, True Teachings, or Provisional Teachings). This is very important. One must try to have a mind of the utmost purity and words and behavior of the utmost virtuousness. EILS

131. Not only do human beings possess the heart of compassion, animals do too. This is truly the virtuous original nature. The nature of animals is no different from ours, but because they are even more deeply deluded than we are, they have been born as animals. All the beings in the Ten Dharma Realms share the same true nature. This is why the Buddha, in the Mahayana sutras, spoke of "unconditional great compassion and the kindness of realizing that we are one entity." CD

132. One is jealous because one cannot bear to see others do well. A person receives something good because this person had cultivated a good cause—this is his or her reward. What is there to be jealous of? If we want good rewards, we only need to plant good

causes. We should know to rejoice at others' meritorious deeds and help them accomplish them. EILS

133. Why can Buddhism resolve all problems? The *Avataṁsaka Sutra* says: "All phenomena are manifested by the mind." This means that all the physical phenomena and mental phenomena in life and the universe, and even abstract concepts, are created by our own minds and have nothing to do with other people. When a thought arises, phenomena will manifest. When the mind is still, no phenomena will manifest. This is natural. It is described as "it is the way it is" in Buddhism. BC

134. Humility enables us to preserve our good rewards. Without it, we will lose what we have accumulated and all of our efforts will have been in vain. We need to rely on humility for it enables us to preserve our goodness. CD

135. People often say that one brings nothing with one at birth and one takes nothing with one at death. When we die, we cannot take anything that we own with us. We must clearly understand this truth. Does

anything we have now belong to us? No! If we think that what we have belongs to us, this is ignorance. What we have we are just using temporarily, like when we stay in a hotel. Nothing belongs to us. If we can thoroughly understand this reality, we will not have greed. We will be at ease regardless of what we encounter in life and will not mind or take anything seriously.

When we understand the truth, we will have peace of mind. When we have peace of mind, we will surely see the truth. Therefore, we should let go of everything that is irrelevant—absolutely give no rise to greed. We should enthusiastically do more good deeds for the sake of all beings and society. EILS

136. People in this world do not understand the truth of life and the universe. They are ignorant and selfish. The Buddha told us the truth of life and the universe—the entire Dharma Realm is one entity, and the true nature of Buddhas and bodhisattvas and that of all beings are one. From this, we realize that we and all the other beings in the entire Dharma Realm are closely knit—when we love ourselves, we will love all

beings; when we help others, we are helping our-selves. EILS

137. Virtually everyone would prefer to be good. Even the worst person will usually say that he or she would like to practice goodness. From this, we can conclude that a good heart and behavior is the true nature of humanity. Buddhism teaches us that this is a virtue of our true nature.

If this is the case, why do people resort to immoral conduct? Two reasons. First, people commit bad deeds because of their afflictions and bad habits. Sec-ond, they do so because of bad conditions. While they are committing bad deeds, most are bothered by their conscience, unfortunately, they do not have any good friends to help them to reform, and so they become more deluded and confused. CD

138. The Buddha divided all activities into three kinds: good, bad, and morally neutral. Morally neutral means that the activity is neither good nor bad. For example, wiping one's face with a towel and drinking a cup of tea are morally neutral activities. TVKS

139. Instead of losing our tempers and becoming angry, we should sincerely reflect and remind ourselves that we are only human and that each of us has faults. If we cannot forgive others' shortcomings, how can we expect them to forgive ours?

Thinking in this manner, we will no longer condemn others but will instead feel empathy for them. People only make mistakes due to their ignorance. They lack the ability to distinguish between true and false, proper and deviated, and between harmful and beneficial. Thus, they cannot correct themselves, end their erroneous ways, or cultivate kindness. We should feel sympathy for them and not be reproachful. In so doing, we follow the Buddha's and bodhisattva's way of relating to people and situations. CD

140. If one cultivates good fortune but loses one's temper often, harbors hatred and jealousy, is arrogant, or loves to outdo others, one will have no merits but will still have great good fortune. This is because good fortune cannot be burned away. Which path will this kind of people be reborn in? The Buddha said that they will be reborn in the path of asuras. Asuras have good fortune but no virtues. They are prone to anger

and lose their temper easily and hurt others. But when they use up their good fortune, they will fall into a bad realm. Buddhism often talks about "anger and resentment in the third lifetime"—one cultivates good fortune in the first lifetime, enjoys it in the second lifetime, and falls into a bad realm in the third lifetime. EILS

141. When a family member is in a crisis, we should recite sutras and a Buddha's name, and then dedicate the merits to all beings throughout the universe. We should wish that all living beings will no longer suffer, but be happy and healthy. When we are sincere in this thought, our family members will gain as well. Why? Because our heart is truly pervasive! CD

142. People often say, "I have dedicated all my merits to others and gained nothing for myself. What is the use in practicing goodness?" This could only come from a narrow mind. If we prostrate in front of the Buddha but do not feel any response, it is because our hearts are selfish. We are totally self-seeking and do not know that we should magnify our merits so that they encompass the entire universe. When we dedi-

cate the merits to all living things, it is like passing on a light. We use our flame to light those of others, so that the whole world is bathed in brightness. This results in great benefit for all with no loss to ourselves. People who practice Buddhism need to dedicate the merits from practice to all living beings in the universe, to awakening, and to reality, in order to uncover the perfect complete true Buddha-nature. CD

143. People in this world do not understand the truth of life and the universe. They are ignorant and selfish. The Buddha told us the truth of life and the universe—the entire Dharma Realm is one entity, and the true nature of Buddhas and bodhisattvas and that of all beings are one. From this, we realize that we and all the other beings in the entire Dharma Realm are closely knit—when we love ourselves, we will love all beings; when we help others, we are helping ourselves. EILS

144. The law of cause and effect, what we often refer to as karma, spans many lifetimes. When someone takes advantage of you financially, you are leaving behind money that is meant for future lifetimes when

it will be paid back. Do not dwell on this matter. Do not hesitate to do good deeds because of these obstacles. Just as we appreciate material things coming to us now, we will likewise appreciate them in the future, whether that future is close or distant. ASC

145. It is most important that as Buddhists, we know exactly why we are practicing—to accumulate the ultimate good fortune for our last moments of life. What is ultimate good fortune? It to know that when our time is up, we can leave this world without illness, in a sitting or a standing position, and that we know exactly where we will be going. This is the greatest good fortune, but most people are unaware of this. Practitioners should constantly remind themselves to share their good fortune with others. That way the good fortune will be even greater. CD

146. Our viewpoints, speech, and behavior all flow from our true nature when we see our true nature. Otherwise, they flow from our afflictions and residual habits.

Our viewpoints, speech, and behavior are still selfish and dictated by our greed, anger, and ignorance.

There is no selfishness or greed, anger, and ignorance in Buddhas' and Dharma-body Mahasattvas' viewpoints, speech, and behavior. We should ask ourselves if we are still selfish, or if we still have greed, anger, ignorance, and arrogance. If we still like this or dislike that, we still have an ego that likes and dislikes.

When we have an ego, then we still have selfishness. Even if there is only a trace of any of those in us, we are not yet awakened. We still have not seen true nature. One who has seen true nature is completely free of selfishness, greed, anger, ignorance, and arrogance. ASC

147. Maitreya is an expert on the consciousness-only teachings. He said that in the arising of thoughts, there are 1.28 x 1015 wave motions in one second. With every wave motion, physical and mental phenomena simultaneously manifest. Think about this. When we watch a movie, twenty-four frames are flashed per second, which already makes us feel that the scenes on the screen are very real. The present universe—the external environment that our six senses come into contact with—appear to us at the super speed of 1.28 x 1015 frames per second. This is

why it is stated in the *Diamond Sutra*: "All phenomena are illusory." This is the truth, not just a description, of all phenomena. BC

148. When we are reborn in the Western Pure Land, our wisdom, capabilities, virtues, and abilities will be uncovered. We will then be able to come back to the Nine Dharma Realms to help those who have an affinity with us. What affinity? Repaying kindness, taking revenge, collecting debts, and repaying debts.

We help those who have these four kinds of affinity with us. As long as there is affinity, with wisdom and expedient means, we will be able to help them end delusion and attain enlightenment, and to help them transform from ordinary people to sages. When we help others achieve these goals, we also achieve in our cultivation of virtues, wisdom, and good fortune. ASC

149. When someone offends us for no reason at all, it is their problem, not ours. If someone attacks us unfairly, it does not concern us. Even if they attack us physically, there is no reason to become angry. This body is not "me." Purity of mind will never be hurt by

attacks, as purity of mind by its nature contains nothing. It is a shame that we do not employ purity of mind when we interact with others or circumstances.

What we use is the illusory mind not the true self. Buddhism teaches us to seek the original self. This true, pure mind does not give rise to any wandering thoughts. Our surroundings will not affect the pure mind. If something does not concern us, why should we worry about it? Why should we be so attached to it? Once we sever all wandering discriminatory thoughts and attachments, what is there to concern us?

Nothing.

By understanding the logic, our minds will be settled and no longer affected by external conditions, and we will achieve perfect peace of mind. Regardless of what happens around us, we can remain calm. When we encounter favorable conditions, we do not give rise to the heart of greed. Encountering unfavorable conditions, we do not give rise to the heart of anger. Regardless of the circumstances, we are able to maintain the mind of purity, equality, and compassion to genuinely reform ourselves. CD

150. The *Platform Sutra* says: "If one is a true practitioner, one will not see the faults of others." Why will one not see the faults of others? Because one regards all dharmas as illusory! There is no fault. There is no merit. No good and no evil. One's mind is impartial: without discrimination or attachment, there is neither good nor evil, neither right nor wrong, and neither true nor false. One will naturally not speak of the faults of others. Therefore, good or evil, right or wrong, and true or false—these are unfounded discriminations formed by people in this world. EILS

151. Modern scientists acknowledge that matter in the universe is generated by waves. The speed of waves is very rapid. This wave originates in the vibration of thoughts.

Matter does not exist. It is an illusory phenomenon of the entangling and accumulation of thoughts. Its foundation is thoughts. Without thoughts, there will be no matter. This conclusion coincides with the teachings in the Buddhist sutras, which say that an unawakened thought is the mark of karma. The mark of karma is a phenomenon of the vibration of thoughts. From vibration manifests the spiritual phenomena and the physical phenomena. Understanding this, we will realize that objects change in accordance with the mind. SC

152. Those who achieve the four dhyanas and the eight concentrations cannot transcend the Six Paths because they are attached to the state of meditative concentration they are in and will not let go of it. Attachment leads to greed, which is still a wandering thought.

This is to remind us to exercise wisdom. We can enjoy the state of meditative concentration but should not be attached to it. If we can achieve this non-attachment, there will be no adverse effects.

It is the same with our present situation. We can enjoy whatever we are experiencing but we should not attach to it. If discriminations and attachments arise in us, then we are wrong and will have trouble. ASC

153. As beings ensnared in the cycle of rebirth, we are all subject to what is called the Eight Sufferings. The first seven—birth, aging, illness, death, separation from loved ones, association with those we dislike,

and unfulfilled desires—are suffering as retribution. The last one, the suffering due to the five aggregates, is a general description.

Where does suffering come from? The Buddha talked about "suffering due to the five aggregates." The five aggregates are form, feeling, conception, impulse, and consciousness. Form refers to the physical body. Feeling, conception, impulse, and consciousness refer to mental activities.

All living beings are made up of these five aggregates. In other words, life is the combination of matter and mind. The body is matter and thus is subject to birth, aging, illness, and death. Mentally, we are subject to the experience of unfulfilled desires, separation from loved ones, and association with those we dislike. ASC

154. Positive and negative karma as well as the entire universe are created from our mind. The Buddha told us in the *Avatamsaka Sutra*: "The nature of the Dharma realms arises from the mind. Nature is essence and essence is the mind." How do Mahayana bodhisattvas enter the hell realms to help the beings there? These enlightened beings do so by understand-

ing the principle that everything arises from the mind. We learn from the *Ksitigarbha Sutra* that to break through the doors of the hells, one needs to understand that everything arises from the mind. What is Hell? A creation of our minds. Understanding this, we will learn that there are no gates to hell—we can come and go freely! CD

155. How can one be truly free of confusion or delusion? Let us observe a truly awakened person. This person has a clear understanding of him- or herself as well as the living environment. Understanding is awakening. What is the standard for understanding?

The Buddha was a truly awakened person. He is our standard. The Buddha said that the truth of this world is "suffering, emptiness, and impermanence." This is the truth of this mundane world. No one can escape from this.

This world is filled with suffering, is empty in nature, and is impermanent. We must clearly understand this. When we do, we should abandon suffering, emptiness, and impermanence in this world and seek the state of permanence, joy, true self, and purity. Achieving this, we are truly awakened. The state of "permanence, joy, true self, and purity" is the state of Buddhas and bodhisattvas. EILS

156. Whether intentional or unintentional, obstructing others or harming others to benefit ourselves is something that we must not do. Our lives are short. When we try to benefit ourselves, how much benefit can we gain and for how long can we enjoy it? And for this, we will have the retribution of falling into the Three Evil Paths. The length of time we suffer there will far exceed the amount of time we spend enjoying those fleeting benefits.

Why would we want to do such a foolish thing? ASC

Cultivation

157. We should be as respectful to non-sentient beings as to Buddhas. For example, tables and chairs are non-sentient beings. Our respect to them should be the same as that to Buddhas, without any difference. This is the practice of Samantabhadra. When we see tables and chairs, we put them in their proper places and keep them clean. This is showing our respect to them. The respect in our hearts is exactly the same, though how we express the respect differs. Practicing respect for all Buddhas starts from this point [the impartial respect for all beings]. EILS

158. Enlightenment is to know and correct our faults. Bodhisattvas are enlightened sentient beings. We are also sentient beings, but are unenlightened since we do not know our faults and thus do not know to correct them. We believe that we are already correct. "Do I have any faults?" we question ourselves, and thinking for a long while we cannot find any. Thus, it is said that ordinary people do not have faults while bodhisattvas have many. They constantly watch over their every thought, word, and deed, knowing that

they have many shortcomings, continuously correcting them and doing so for three great eons. When we think about how many faults there can be, how can we possibly think that as ordinary people we do not have any! CD

159. Respect—everything should start with it, not just when we are learning the supreme Buddhadharma. "Single-minded respect"—we often read these words in the repentance section that appears in the Buddhist practice book. Single-mindedness is the practice of Samantabhadra. It signifies impartiality. Single-mindedness is maintaining the same mind whether we encounter Buddhas, people, animals, or tables and chairs. With two minds, differences and discrimination arise. Therefore, with two minds or three minds, we are not quite respectful and not following the practice of Samantabhadra. We must clearly understand this before we know how to learn. EILS

160. The Buddha's teaching is the most wondrous and virtuous teaching in this world and beyond. Wherever the Buddha's teaching is propagated, whether in a country, a city, or a village, if the people can follow his

teachings and practice diligently, there will be good learning results: transforming from an ordinary being into a sage, transforming suffering into happiness, and transforming greed, anger, and ignorance into precept observation, meditative concentration, and wisdom. What will be shown is that "the world would be in harmony and accordance." The entire universe can be in harmony and conformity. SC

161. To achieve in our practice, we need to let go of worldly concerns. Letting go does not mean that we do not care and will not help. We care, extend our help and let go simultaneously. This is wisdom. Those who care but cannot let go are still ruled by emotions.

How do Buddhas and bodhisattvas manage to care, help, and let go? They have true wisdom. They have turned all their emotions into wisdom, which is the ultimate perfect wisdom. They have wondrous and amazing flexibility and skills. Although they help all beings out of great compassion, there is no slightest attachment in their minds. This is the wonderful working of innate virtues. ASC

162. Changing our conduct and improving ourselves is true cultivation. It is by no means just a formality of reciting sutras, prostrating before the Buddha, or chanting mantras. To have cultivated an entire lifetime and still be mired in the cycle of rebirth is to have simply gone through the formalities. For others, formalities exemplify the teachings so that they might see them and begin to awaken. For us, they serve as reminders of the teachings.

For self-cultivation however, importance is not placed on the formalities but rather on discovering our faults. This is awakening. To correct our faults is to improve in our cultivation. Therefore, the most important point is for us to be calm, introspective, and be watchful of our conduct as we look for our bad habits and faults. When we know these, we will know where to begin, what to correct, and how to proceed. We can then concentrate and use all of our energy to reform. CD

163. The more one achieves in practice, the more wisdom one will have. The more wisdom one has, the deeper is one's belief and thus the more one will achieve in practice. As one achieves more in practice,

one will have even more wisdom. This is how meditative concentration and wisdom complement each
other perpetually. When one practices this way, one
will transcend all evil paths. EILS

164. Sakyamuni Buddha attained enlightenment and
Buddhahood at the age of thirty. After he had attained
Buddhahood, he started to propagate the Dharma and
benefit all beings. He did so for forty-nine years until
he entered nirvana at eighty.

During the forty-nine years, Sakyamuni did not
have a day off. Why? Because what he taught—ending the cycle of rebirth and transcending the Three
Realms—was very important. So he could not take
any day off. Had he done so, his students' learning
would have been interrupted, and they would have
regressed. Learning is like going upstream in a boat; if
you do not move forward, you go backward. It is the
same in cultivation; if one does not make progress,
one immediately regresses. ASC

165. Once the mind is pure, all obstacles that prevent
us from obtaining good fruits from our cultivation will
be eliminated, and one will stay away from the evil

paths. When one is free of anger, one will transcend the door of hells. When one is free of ignorance, one will transcend the door of animals. When one is free of greed and miserliness, one will transcend the door of hungry ghosts. Therefore, when one eradicates greed, anger, and ignorance, one will transcend the Three Evil Paths. And if one does not have the slightest yearning for the good fortune in the human and heavenly paths, one will transcend the Six Paths. EILS

166. Virtue, morality, kindness, and integrity are on the inside and are the cultivation of virtuous conduct. Fame, wealth, and prestige are on the outside and are the enjoyments in life. To be able to receive both kinds of benefits is of great value. As is said in the *Avatamsaka Sutra*, "not to be hindered in the matter of phenomena or principles" is the ultimate and perfect enjoyment. This is the great perfection of everything going as we wish, when we are satisfied with everything. This is to be liberated; it is to do all that is benevolent and noble as we wish. CD

167. Giving is letting go—letting go of everything in this world. All the afflictions, even illnesses, birth and death, and the root cause of transmigration come about because one is unwilling to let go of wandering thoughts and attachments. One truly reaps the fruit of one's actions. The purpose of giving is to help one let go of one's concerns, worries, afflictions, wandering thoughts, discriminations, and attachments. EILS

168. In reforming, we need to have shame, fear, and courageous determination. To have a shameful heart is to be awakened. To have a respectful and fearful heart is to be conscience-stricken. Only when we have both of these, do we give rise to the courageous and determined heart that enables us to regret and reform.

Realizing this, why are we unable to correct our faults? Since we have yet to possess a shameful and fearful heart, we do not have the motivation that gives rise to a courageous and determined heart. If we do not know shame, then we will not be afraid of being laughed at by others so there is little incentive for us to cultivate kindness. CD

169. Patience is forbearance. The *Prajna Sutra* says: "All accomplishments are attributed to patience." Therefore, patience requires resolute endurance. Considerable patience is needed for any accomplishment in worldly undertakings, let alone in learning Buddhism. One must be able to exercise patience. When one is patient, one will be able to maintain a tranquil mind and advance in one's cultivation. If one is not patient, one will not have any progress in one's cultivation no matter how diligently one cultivates. Patience requires true effort. It is a prerequisite for meditative concentration. EILS

170. To acknowledge all of one's offenses without hiding anything is to regret and eradicate one's karmic obstacles. This must be done sincerely to be effective. Awakening is achieved when we are able to identify our faults. Cultivation is accomplished when we have realized these faults and corrected them. Since most people are unaware of their mistakes, they are not truly cultivating. Therefore, the first step is to recognize our bad habits. CD

171. When one has meditative concentration and wisdom, one has great benefit. Meditative concentration and wisdom come forth when the true mind is active. As a result, one is able to control one's destiny anywhere in the universe. When one does not have meditative concentration and wisdom, one is controlled by affliction and temptation. This is pitiable.

Therefore, cultivation is nothing but this: internally, ridding oneself of greed, anger, and ignorance; and externally, cutting off all temptations. EILS

172. Even the highest-level Bodhisattvas still have faults. What kind? They still have one degree of ignorance yet to be broken through. If Equal-enlightenment Bodhisattvas still need to regret and reform, we can imagine how much we need to do! From now on, we need to have the compassionate heart to feel remorse and change for the better. Even upon reaching the level of Equal-enlightenment Bodhisattvas, we will still need to do this. Only when there is nothing left to correct will we become Buddhas. We cannot attain supreme enlightenment if we still have one remaining fault. CD

173. The Ten Virtuous Karmas are more profound and extensive than the Five Precepts. The Five Precepts are the Buddha's teaching to his students. The Ten Virtuous Karmas are the Buddha's teaching to all the beings, teachings that we should abide by in daily life, at work, in engaging in a task, interaction with people, and dealing with a situation. TVKS

174. The basic educational goals in Confucianism are to sever material desires, obtain awakening, uphold a sincere mind and a virtuous heart, develop self-discipline, have a harmonious family, govern a country, and foster world peace. Today, schools do not emphasize these principles or the humanities, but stress technology. No wonder our thoughts and behavior have no guiding principles. We are not taught that when we see the misdeeds of others, we are to take a hard look at ourselves and see if we have fulfilled our duties as leaders. CD

175. The gravest offense of all is killing; the greatest obstacle to one's cultivation is sexual desire. These are two great obstacles. If in one's cultivation one wishes to transcend this world, one will not be able to tran-

scend the Three Realms without eradicating sexual desire. EILS

176. Instead of losing our tempers and becoming angry, we should sincerely reflect and remind ourselves that we are only human and that each of us has faults. If we cannot forgive others' shortcomings, how can we expect them to forgive ours? Thinking in this manner, we will no longer condemn others but will instead feel empathy for them. People only make mistakes due to their ignorance. They lack the ability to distinguish between true and false, proper and deviated, and between harmful and beneficial. Thus, they cannot correct themselves, end their erroneous ways, or cultivate kindness. We should feel sympathy for them and not be reproachful. In so doing, we follow the Buddha's and bodhisattva's way of relating to people and situations. CD

177. If our every thought is of ourselves, ego-attachment will worsen day by day. How then can we transcend the Three Realms? This is why the Buddha taught us to always think of benefiting all beings. This way, the thoughts of benefiting ourselves will gradu-

ally diminish and go away. Our every thought and every deed should be for all beings, not for ourselves. When all beings have good fortune, we too have good fortune, because we are also one of the beings. Similarly, we cannot avoid misfortune if all beings have misfortune. EILS

178. Confucius taught loving-kindness, explaining, "The benevolent person has no enemies." If we cannot accept anything that is contrary to what we think, then we are neither kind nor compassionate. Conflict simply does not exist within the heart of loving-kindness. This is also what is meant in Buddhism as great compassion and is what we need to learn and practice to truly benefit ourselves. CD

179. We often hurt others with our careless speech. Those we hurt may take offense and bear grudges, and in the future will seek revenge. Thus, many problems are created out of misunderstandings, and resentments arise because of what we have said. "The speaker had no such intention, the listener interpreted it to be so." We need to be careful and restrained in

our speech. And frankly, there is no need to talk a lot. In talking less, we will commit fewer mistakes. CD

180. Like Confucianism, Buddhism is also founded on filial piety to one's parents and respect for one's teachers. Confucian teaching flourished because of this foundation, as did the Buddha's teaching. Filial piety is thus very important, for only when one is filial will one respect teachers. If one truly respects one's teachers, one will receive the Way taught by the teachers. If one does not respect one's teachers, they will not be able to teach one anything no matter how good they are. Why? Because one will not believe them nor be willing to learn from them. When one respects one's teachers, one will listen to their teaching and diligently practice accordingly. One will thus receive the merits and benefits. Respecting one's teachers is respecting the Way and receiving it. EILS

181. We should not attach to formalities in our practice. For example, those who are older and less agile do not need to kneel when reciting a sutra. To seek a bond between Buddha Amitabha and ourselves is of the utmost importance. We can continue our practice

even when lying down. The weak or aged can use the most comfortable position while chanting "Amituofo" or reciting the sutra, be it kneeling, sitting, or walking. If weak, we can lie down and listen to the sutra on a tape. Lying in bed listening to the sutra or chanting "Amituofo" can achieve the same merits as when we are sitting or walking. CD

182. Zhangjia Living Buddha taught that because life is short and full of suffering, one must end wrongdoings and practice virtuous conduct, accumulate merits and cultivate virtues, and should not compete with others or crave anything. These are the key guidelines that he taught me.

Therefore, when someone competes with me for something, I will yield to this person. I have been learning to exercise forbearance and to allow others to take advantage of me. Why do I do this? Because allowing others to take advantage of me brings me good fortune. This is true! Every time I yield or allow others to take advantage of me, I end up having wonderful consequences. I have always advanced to a higher level in every aspect, and my state of mind has improved. Therefore, I have become more and more

confident in the teachings of my teachers, bodhisattvas, and Buddhas. ASC

183. In learning Buddhism, one needs only to cultivate a pure mind. When one has a pure mind, one will
naturally be impartial and enlightened. At all times, in
all places, and in all situations, whether favorable or
adverse, one needs to maintain a pure and uncontami-
nated mind. The mind will naturally be pure when (1)
internally, greed, anger, ignorance, and arrogance do
not arise in one, and (2) externally, one is not attached
to any environment, good or bad. A pure mind is the
true mind and is true wisdom. When handling any
situation, one will do it correctly and completely,
without any mistakes. All mistakes arise from desire
and thoughts of gain and loss. EILS

184. We can correct our faults by beginning to change
from our minds and practicing good deeds. If we
practice from our minds, then even a small good deed
such as unreservedly giving a penny to a person in
need would be of infinite merits and virtues. Why?
This deed comes from the great compassion in our
true nature, thus the broadmindedness is boundless.

The good fortune is infinite for the good deed arises from our minds and accords with our true nature. However, if the good deed arises solely from our actions, then it is a small merit for it did not arise from our true nature. CD

185. In engaging in a task, interacting with people, dealing with a situation, in daily life or at work, remember that allowing others to take advantage of one will bring one good fortune. One must not have the thought of taking advantage of others. If one tries to take advantage of others, one will suffer great loss. When one has the thought of taking advantage of others, one is transgressing the precept of no stealing. TVKS

186. We should do our best to perform deeds that will benefit others. Maybe there is a limit to what we can do, but if we perform deeds with a sincere, respectful, and pure mind and with patience, we will have the support of Buddhas and bodhisattvas. Our wishes will surely be fulfilled. EILS

187. Along the path of cultivation, there are many obstacles. As in a race, we all start at the same starting
line, but some progress ahead of others, some lag behind, and some are eliminated. Why? Because there
are many obstacles. The obstacles may be people or
situations. They may be our family, friends, or those
we have hurt in the past and owe karmic debts to.

Who can overcome all these obstacles and progress in their practice? Those who single-mindedly
concentrate on cultivation. In our practice, we recite
the Buddha's name or our selected sutra every day.
We also study the teachings every day. If we are very
busy with work and family responsibilities, we can at
least chant and study for a few minutes. The main
thing is to practice and study every day. ASC

188. In doing any deed, no matter how small, one
should dedicate the merit accrued to all beings, wishing that all suffering beings could leave suffering behind and attain happiness. This is a form of Dharma
offerings: by giving of ourselves for all beings.

One does not personally enjoy the good fortune
one has cultivated but shares it with all beings. This is
the meaning of dedication. One shares one's wisdom,

good fortune, skills, and abilities with all beings, wishing that all beings could have peace and happiness. This is a bodhisattva practice.

Can this be done? Yes. If one truly practices, others will benefit. If these people are about to encounter a disaster, and there is someone who has great good fortune and merits, either they will not encounter the disaster or the severity of the disaster will be reduced. EILS

189. If we conceal our faults, they will increase at an alarming rate. If we are smart, we will let them be known. Then, when we are criticized and corrected, our karmic obstacles will be gradually eradicated. If others speak out about our mistakes, be grateful even if we have not done what they said we did, for to be wrongly accused by others will also eradicate our karmic obstacles. There is no need to refute or defend ourselves in the face of undeserved accusations. When we are defensive, others will not want to help us correct our faults. Then the offense will become even more serious. CD

190. Although one's destiny is predetermined, it changes every day in accordance with one's behavior. So, can one change one's destiny? Yes, one can. If one's behavior every day adds a little to or subtracts a little from good fortune—by one doing small good acts and committing small bad acts—then one's life will be governed by one's destiny, and there will be no change. But if one does major deeds—either good or evil—then one's destiny will be changed.

Therefore, one's destiny after one is forty years old is greatly influenced by one's behavior in this lifetime. One's destiny before one is forty years old is predetermined, greatly influenced by one's good and evil deeds done in past lifetimes. If one is truly awakened and diligently ends wrongdoings and practices virtuous conduct, one's destiny will change for the better after one is forty years old. This is very important. EILS

191. Illnesses come from the mind and behavior that are not virtuous. It is brought about by negative karmas committed out of greed, anger, ignorance, and afflictions. The ancient Chinese said: "Worry can age a person." Medical science has now found that losing

one's temper is the same as gradually committing suicide. When one's every thought accords with the Three Poisons and the Ten Evil Karmas, the whole body—blood, bones, flesh, and cells—will change for the worse. This is the cause of illnesses.

If we receive the teaching of the Buddha and the sages every day, and we maintain a sincere, pure, impartial, compassionate, loving, and joyous mind, every cell in our bodies will be healthy. How then can we get sick?

From this we can see that constantly having compassion, love, and gratitude in our heart is truly the most important factor for physical and mental well-being, a harmonious relationship with others, and a harmonious environment. BC

192. If one is truly awakened, one will naturally be unperturbed in any situation and one can enter very deep meditative concentration—being unperturbed is achieving meditative concentration. When one's mind is not perturbed, one will truly understand all phenomena. This understanding is wisdom. Being free of discrimination and attachment is meditative concentration. When we have both meditative concentration

and wisdom, meditative concentration and wisdom are perfect and complete. This is the place where we start to cultivate meditative concentration and wisdom. This is real. EILS

193. Making offerings to infinite sages is also a great virtuous deed. But, we learn from the *Infinite Life Sutra* that it is even better to turn back from delusion and to conscientiously cultivate. Cultivation is to change ourselves. The ancient sages regarded it as the great virtue of regretting and reforming. CD

194. These situations—someone says charming words to us but we do not attach to the words, or someone tries to stir up trouble but we feel no anger—help us to cultivate and attain meditative concentration and wisdom. One Mind Undisturbed and the Buddha-name Chanting Samadhi taught in Pure Land Buddhism are both attained in this way. If one's mind is perturbed by others gossiping or passing rumors about us, one should immediately feel remorse: "I am wrong again. I am affected by the external environment again." EILS

195. Can society be saved? The answer is most definitely positive. But saved by whom? We have to take this as our responsibility right now. "It is my responsibility to save the world." There is no difference between myself and the world—the world and I are one. Only when I can let go of all my selfish thoughts, my thoughts of greed, anger, ignorance, and arrogance, can I eliminate the disasters in this world and calm the Earth's climate. When I can truly let go of all conflicts against all people and the environment, will our world will be harmonious and peaceful. Therefore, we need to have a great bodhi mind, a great compassionate mind.   WPH

196. An ancient eminent master said, "[When we die,] we cannot take anything with us; only karmas will accompany us." Fame and honor, wealth and rank, and money and possessions—we cannot take these with us. All the good karmas and bad karmas created in our lifetime will stay with us. Those who are truly awakened know that they should cultivate what they can take with them. What they cannot take along, they should just ignore and waste no energy on them. EILS

197. We can choose whichever method best fits our manner of living and level of achievement and understanding. The most important point is to concentrate on just one method. The more methods we try to follow, the more confused we will become. The more confused we are, the more difficult it is to succeed. This is very important, as samadhi or deep concentration, is the key to success in our learning and cultivation. BACW

198. Confucius often said: "In every group of three people, there is teacher we can learn from." When we include ourselves in a group of three, there will be one person who is more virtuous and one who is less virtuous. We emulate the former and observe the latter to see if we have the same faults. If so, we quickly correct them. In this way, we learn from both examples. AL

199. What is the difference between "enlightened" and "unenlightened"? One who knows that they have many faults is an enlightened being—a bodhisattva. One who does not know they possess numerous faults is unenlightened—an ordinary person. CD

200. Wealth is good fortune, and it will be used up some day. It is stated in the sutras that one's wealth belongs to five families. The first is water, which can flood one's properties. The second is fire, which can burn one's properties. The third is the government. In the past, the government would confiscate all the properties of a criminal. The fourth is robbers and thieves. The fifth is spendthrift children, who are hard to guard against. EILS

201. The Buddha has taught us to let go of all desires and greed. He did not ask us to turn to new objects for our greed. In the past, we sought worldly joys, now we seek and attach to Buddhist knowledge. The mind of greed is still there. Therefore, whether for worldly life or for Buddhist knowledge, we would do well not to be greedy. Greed is the source of all misdeeds and wrongdoing. BACW

202. "The sincere and honest heart" is the essence of the eight guidelines taught by Confucius. We accomplish this by severing our desires and uncovering our true nature. Failing to do this, we will be unable to accomplish ultimate sincerity. When severing desires,

what are we cutting off? The Six Dusts or polluting factors of sight, hearing, smell, taste, touch, and thought and the Five Desires for wealth, sex, fame, food, and sleep. If these desires cannot be reduced, our hearts will be constantly affected by our surroundings. How can such a heart remain sincere? CD

203. Chinese Buddhists primarily practice Mahayana Buddhism and wish to develop the bodhi mind, the awakened mind that is genuinely free from delusions and that realizes this world is filled with suffering. It is the compassionate and sincere mind, with every thought to attain realization for self and others. The Buddha told us that suffering exists throughout the six realms, including the human and heaven realms. In the human realm can be summarized as the Eight Sufferings of birth, old age, sickness, death, hardships, the inability to have what we want, separation from those we love, and association with those we dislike. BACW

204. Deep concentration is the state of constantly maintaining a mind of purity and equality. Cultivating deep concentration does not solely mean sitting in

meditation in the cultivation hall. Practicing sitting meditation is similar to teaching the skills to a beginner. After graduation from school, the students need to practice what they have learned in the cultivation hall by applying the principles in their daily lives. The practitioner will have practiced deep concentration when he or she can remain unaffected by external circumstances. AL

205. The first stage [in cultivation] is belief. When we are able to believe then our conditions have matured. There is a saying "the Buddha is unable to help those who have no affinity with him." What is affinity? It is being able to believe. Even a Buddha cannot help someone whose conditions have not yet matured. But when they have matured, the person will have belief. Then the Buddha can help. Religions are different from Buddhism in that once the believers have faith, they are saved. Belief in Buddhism means that we believe in the benefits of Buddhism and accept one of the many methods. BACW

206. In order to gain, we must first let go. If we are reluctant to let go, then we will not be able to gain. In

the sutras, we read that to give is to gain. We first give up something in order to gain something in return. Without giving, we will receive nothing. So, this lesson on reforming our destinies is all about letting go. What if we seek something? To seek also helps us to receive. But how do we accomplish this? Just let go and we will receive everything we are seeking. CD

207. We need to know the proper sequence of cultivation: belief, understanding, practice, and attainment. When we speak of belief, first we believe in ourselves. This is where Buddhism differs from religion. In religion, the most important criteria is to believe in God. In Buddhism, the most important criteria is to believe in ourselves, not something outside of ourselves. We need to believe that we have the same Buddha nature. Believe that originally we were Buddhas. Believe that we are no different from the Buddhas. Believe that our true nature has become polluted and that once we remove this pollution we will uncover our true nature. BACW

208. It is essential for us to learn modesty for it is the key to cultivating and improving our virtue. We need

to realize that others are better than us and that they excel in what they do. When we are false and conceited, other people may not see this; however, Buddhas, bodhisattvas, and the beings and spirits of heaven and earth see us very clearly. Thus, our modesty must be sincere and come from deep within.

We are not better than others and if they accumulate merits and we do not, then they are better than us. Even when we dare not commit offenses, others are still better than us. This is perfect modesty and it is the practice of the teaching of humility in the *Avatamsaka Sutra*. I am the only student; everyone else is my teacher. CD

209. Every aspect in one's life should be simple. Simplicity leads to a long life. The ancient Chinese often said, "Illness enters through the mouth." Nowadays, many people contract strange illnesses, which come mostly from the food consumed. In the past in China, there were people in the countryside who maintained a simple diet, but they were healthy and lived a long life. This proves that the simpler the food, the healthier one is. A pure mind with no wandering thoughts, a regular routine, a simple diet, few desires, and con-

tentment—these are the essentials for good health. EILS

210. In the past, practitioners ate one meal a day. Mr. Li ate a meal before noon every day. His work load was the same as that of five people. but he needed only one meal, and he ate very little at that. Why? Because he had very few wandering thoughts, discriminations, and attachments, and thus used very little energy. ASC

211. After we have belief in ourselves, we need to have belief in the Buddha's teachings. Great Master Ouyi described this as believing in principles and in matter. Where does matter come from? From the principle, that is the pure mind of the true nature. All phenomena in the universe arise from the principle. They are related by the endless cycle of cause and effect.

A cause gives rise to an effect, which in turn becomes the cause of the next effect. This process continues ceaselessly. Developing understanding and belief in true reality builds our confidence enabling us to seek thorough understanding of everything. Only in this way can we be free from confusion and doubt, which are obstacles in our cultivation, and obtain enjoyment and smooth advancement. BACW

212. Being gluttonous and stingy—residual habits from countless kalpas—are great obstacles to the practice of giving and must be overcome. One should live a thrifty life and maintain this simple life. Even when one becomes successful and has great wealth in the future, one should still live thriftily. This way, one will truly have good fortune. EILS

213. How then do we reform ourselves from our minds? We sincerely cultivating by wanting to correct our offenses, practicing goodness, and refraining from wrongdoings. When we correct from our minds, there is no such thing as should or should not. Reforming ourselves by reasoning and realizing the principle is conditional. However, when we reform from the mind, it is unconditional, pure, and sincere. In this way, giving rise to even the slightest of kind thoughts will be in harmony with our true nature. Knowing that everything arises from the mind, we need to correct our faults by beginning from the mind. CD

214. Since sentient beings have not yet found their true nature, we teach them to end their erroneous ways and cultivate good deeds. When we have uncovered our true nature, there will be no erroneous ways to be ended and no good deeds to be cultivated, for our minds will be in a state of purity and equality—the One True Dharma Realm—the state of non-cultivation and non-attainment. Within such states, we still do whatever is needed for cultivation and attainment. But, we do not attach to either extreme of emptiness or existence. CD

215. To change karmic retributions and resolve all disasters, I often use a tree as an example. The mind is the root, our thoughts are the trunk, our behavior is the branches, and our speech is the leaves. If we try to correct the problem of an unhealthy tree by plucking off each leaf while forgetting to treat the root, our efforts will be futile. But if we were to begin from the root, to understand from the basics, our problems would be easily solved. AL

216. I am grateful to Ms. Han Yin, who helped me for thirty years. During those years, she helped me have

the opportunity to lecture on stage every day. She was a true Dharma protector. I am grateful to her from the bottom of my heart for my present achievement. Without the thirty years of lecturing experience on stage every day, how could I have any achievement? . .

She then passed away. I will always remember her and feel gratitude to her. How do I repay her kindness? With my achievement. This is the only way I can repay her kindness. ASC

217. It is much better to practice goodness without letting anybody know and even better if some people reproached us, for this will help to reduce our negative karma. It would be best if our negative karma and retributions were reduced and even eradicated, while our merits and virtues remained unknown. CD

218. Why did the Buddha not simply tell us with what we need to know? He did. But we did not listen. We were told the method, but thought to ourselves, "Well this may not be a good method. I heard that another one is better." We have thus argued with the Buddhas and bodhisattvas. So, they have chosen not to come to

us. Please carefully consider this. We need to be very patient before we can attain achievement. Without patience, we cannot advance to a higher stage, for patience is the prerequisite for meditative concentration and diligence. BACW

219. When we find ourselves subjected to hearing gossip, we would just respond with Amituofo. If they gossip more, then again say, "Amituofo." Let them hear this several times. After they are finished talking, we will have listened but disregarded what they said. We will only have said "Amituofo" to them. This is good for it is best not to say much. CD

220. When one has few desires and is content, one's afflictions will reduce and be lighter. Every day, it is enough for one to have a full stomach, adequate clothing, and a place to shield one from wind and rain. A content person is often happy. When one is content, one will want few things. The less one wants, the more at ease and the happier one is. If one truly does not compete with others or crave anything, one will be happier than a celestial being. EILS

221. Great Master Yinguang aptly said that whether or not one achieves in one's learning depends on how sincere and respectful one is. If one is insincere or disrespectful, one will achieve little. ASC

222. When people verbally abuse, criticize, and slander us, we should accept it with a grateful heart rather than a vengeful heart. Why? They have provided us with invaluable assistance that can help us reflect and correct our mistakes immediately if we do have these faults, or guard against them if we do not. If we are not at fault, do not blame these people; instead be encouraged to make further improvements. CD

223. There are three categories of patience. First, tolerate the injuries of physical and verbal abuse. Patience is a virtue. With patience, we will have a quiet and pure mind; thus, it will be easier to attain meditative concentration and achievement. When we successfully practice patience, we will gain the greatest good fortune.

Second, be patient with variations of the natural elements, hot and cold, summer and winter, hunger and thirst, as well as natural disasters.

Third, be patient in the arduous course of our practice. Before we attain the joy of cultivation and our cultivation becomes strong, we will encounter many obstacles. However, once we get through this phase, we will attain happiness. BACW

224. After the sixth Patriarch of Zen, Master Huineng, became enlightened, circumstances found him acting as an attendant to a group of hunters. Daily, he witnessed their hunting and killing. He served meat and cared for them. The hunters were his masters; he was their servant. He did this for not just a short time, but for fifteen years.

Could we have endured this? He not only endured, but was contented and did not have any wandering thoughts, discriminations, or attachments. These were fifteen years of true cultivation. He reached enlightenment when he was in Huangmei, in the southern part of China. Whether under favorable or adverse circumstances, he cultivated his mind of purity, equality, great compassion, and loving-kindness. There is nothing more important to our cultivation than these four virtues, and these were what he practiced. CD

225. Four kinds of karmic links exist between children and parents. The first is to repay kindness. In past lifetimes, they had a good and happy relationship with one another. The children come to repay kindness, so they are very filial.

The second is to exact revenge. The children are karmic debtors from past lifetimes. They are usually wastrels. When they grow up, they will cause the families ruin.

The third is to collect debt. It all depends on how much the parents had owed the children. If the parents did not owe much [previously], the children will die young. If the parents owed the children a lot, the parents will spend a lot of money on the children's education and take very good care of them, and the children will suddenly die when they are adults.

The fourth is to repay debt. The children owed the parents in past lifetimes. When the amount is a lot, the children will look after their parents very attentively.

If the children's debt is little, they will take care of their parents just enough to ensure that their parents lack nothing. But there is no respect for their parents—the children only take care of their physical needs.

When these four kinds of karmic links exist between people, they will become family. People will become relatives or friends when the karmic link is weaker. When the link is stronger, people will become family. EILS

226. A student once asked me, "I am confused by so many methods. Which one do you think I should choose?"

At the time, there happened to be a ball on the ground, which I pointed to and said, "Look at this ball. The surface has points countless as the number of methods. The teachings require you to find the center of the ball. You can reach it from any point on the surface as long as you follow a straight line. You need not find a second or a third point for as an old saying goes, 'Follow the road and you will get home. There is no need to circle around.'"

He then understood that Buddhism pursues the true mind. Once we attain enlightenment, we attain everything. Therefore, no matter which method we choose, the key to success is concentration on one method. So long as we adhere to our chosen method, we will achieve deep concentration, attain wisdom, and uncover the True Nature of Great Perfection. BACW

227. How does one show by example? By practicing according to the teachings. If we teach people to act one way but we ourselves act another way and do not practice what we teach, then those who listen to us may not believe our words. For example, if I tell you to mindfully chant the Buddha-name and I do not do so myself, would you believe my words? You would not.

One must practice what one teaches. This is "show by example." One is not putting on a show; one understands the teachings and principles in the sutras and actually practices them fully. One does what the Buddha teaches one to do and does not do what the Buddha teaches not to do. EILS

228. It is a wandering thought to hope for an early harvest of rewards for our goodness, for such thinking can create obstacles. We are only to ask about the cultivation, not the harvest. As long as we diligently cultivate, the harvest will naturally follow, why bother to constantly seek it? This is the true way of cultivation:

to not seek anything. Just concentrate on ending improper behavior and cultivating goodness; eventually, we will obtain whatever we desire.

When we seek, our gains are limited, for most likely we will only receive what we request, as our cultivation of virtues is not in accordance with our virtuous natures. Without seeking, everything is a manifestation of and in accordance with our virtuous natures. CD

229. There are two approaches in learning Buddhism. The first is practice—here one starts with cultivating a pure mind. The other is understanding—here one studies the teachings. Which approach is more advantageous? Practice. As long as one has a pure mind, it does not matter that one has no knowledge of Buddhism. If one eradicates affliction, then the mind is pure and the Buddha Land will also be pure. One will be able to attain rebirth in the Western Pure Land. EILS

230. If we wish to attain wealth, we practice the giving of wealth. To attain intelligence and wisdom, we practice the giving of teaching. To attain health and

longevity, we practice the giving of fearlessness. This is the correct way to change our destinies. By following the right principles and methods, we can even attain Supreme Enlightenment much less worldly enjoyment and happiness. CD

231. It is said, "A sheep dies and is reborn a human; a human dies and is reborn a sheep." In this life you are the human and you are stronger than the sheep; you kill and eat it. In the next life, the sheep becomes the human and you become the sheep; he will kill and eat you. Each one, in turn, pays back. This is "alternately harming and killing one another." Such agony!

The weak being the prey of the strong is an abnormal phenomenon. It is a malicious relationship—one of continual reprisals. In addition, when one takes revenge, one will not do it in the exact amount—one will overdo it a little. Therefore, the enmity will continue lifetime after lifetime without end and will never be resolved. The retributions will become more and more terrible. EILS

232. All Buddhas symbolize our virtuous nature. All bodhisattvas and arhats symbolize the virtue of prac-

tice. Without the virtue of practice, the innate virtuous nature cannot be revealed. This complementary relationship is why the Buddha table includes both Buddha and bodhisattva images. The Buddhas represent original nature and the bodhisattvas represent the application of this nature and form. This original nature is empty, as it has no set form. All creations or form arise from this original nature and once there is form, there is application. BACW

233. To know our faults daily is to awaken daily. Once we discover a fault, we sincerely correct it; this is how we will build our strength of cultivation. We need not do much. If we were to find and correct one fault a day then we would become a sage or virtuous person in three years. CD

234. We understand the truth, so we should feel empathy for all beings—we should love them, not harm them. What is the cause of wars in this world? The Buddha told us that it is killing. Therefore, if wars are to end forever, beings should not eat meat. EILS

235. The *Vimalakirti Sutra* tells us that "a sincere heart is a cultivation place, a pure heart is a cultivation place, and a compassionate heart is a cultivation place." A proper cultivation place is within our hearts. When our minds are on the path to enlightenment then no matter where we are, there will always be a place for cultivation. CD

Three Learnings

236. In order for us to resolve disasters, the ultimate method is to "cultivate precepts, meditative concentration, and wisdom; cease creating and destroy greed, anger, and ignorance." All forms of prayers, although effective, are not the final solution. Only by universally spreading the teachings of morality, virtue, and causality, can we ultimately transform people's minds and help to solve all the complex problems on Earth. REN

237. When the Buddha taught all beings, his aim was for people to achieve the Three Learnings of precepts, meditative concentration, and wisdom. Abiding by the precepts leads to the achievement of meditative concentration. And from meditative concentration, wisdom arises. Meditative concentration is pivotal to one's learning and cultivation of Buddhism. Abiding by the precepts is the means to achieve meditative concentration. Meditative concentration is the means to uncover wisdom. Uncovering wisdom is the true objective because only wisdom can help us solve all problems. EILS

238. Buddhism teaches us to work to eliminate greed, hatred, and ignorance; to abide by precepts, practice meditative concentration and wisdom; to eliminate all the conflicts within ourselves against all people and environment; to let go of all selfish thoughts; and to only consider the needs of others. If we can truly learn this principle, we are "seeing through" to the truth. But we need to start by putting these teachings into real practice by completely letting go of all greed, anger, ignorance, and arrogance; eradicating all evil and practicing all good deeds; and practicing giving and patience. Doing so we will accumulate merit and virtue. WPH

239. When the Buddha was in our world, he was joyful and open-minded, whether taking part in daily life or teaching and it was this joy and energy that attracted people and helped them to accept Buddhadharma. Buddhadharma is not meant to bind us, but to benefit all beings by bringing them joy and happiness. The formation of the precepts was to show us the right path to attain a happy and fulfilling life. BACW

240. What are the sufferings of the sentient beings in our current age? The first is committing the wrongdoings of the Ten Evil Karmas. The Buddha taught us the First Learning of precepts to overcome these. The second suffering is the inability to remain serene and at peace. The Buddha taught us the Second Learning of meditative concentration to achieve purity of mind and tranquility. The third suffering is ignorance. The Buddha taught us the Third Learning of wisdom to overcome our current state of ignorance. BACW

241. The Buddha told us that if we can abide by the precepts and laws, we would have a tranquil body and mind that will enable us to be free from worries and fears. Since, deep concentration arises from tranquility, the precepts are essential to self-cultivation. If we break the law or the precepts, then our consciences will be plagued by guilt even we are not punished. Moreover, even if we avoid worldly retributions, there is no way to avoid our karmic retributions. When the body and mind are disturbed, we cannot concentrate on our practice and to practice successfully, we need to be tranquil. It is said, "Precepts or self-discipline

lead to deep concentration, from which wisdom arises." BACW

242. Once we have developed a pure and quiet mind, and have attained wisdom, we can begin to broaden our knowledge. We can see, hear, and learn of anything that we are interested in, for now we have attained wisdom and will not be affected by our surroundings. Since we have self-control, the more we see and hear the wiser we will become, and the greater our strength from deep concentration will be. How are deep concentration and wisdom increased? Remaining unmoved by surroundings will enhance deep concentration. Developing a clear and understanding mind will enhance wisdom. Then we can learn from other schools to enhance our deep concentration and wisdom. First, we practice precepts, concentration, and wisdom to attain our original wisdom. Then we can learn extensively to perfect our acquired wisdom. This is the way of learning from ancient times. BACW

Three Refuges

243. When we take refuge in the Three Jewels, we first return to and rely upon the Buddha. For uncountable eons, we have been wandering helplessly and miserably in the six realms. Now we have met a good teacher who shows us that we need to return from our delusion and erroneous thinking, and to rely upon the awakening of our true nature that was originally awakened. So, the Buddha that we rely upon is not to be found outside of ourselves but is innate to our true nature. BACW

244. Taking refuge in the Buddha means being awakened and not deluded. Taking refuge in the Dharma means being proper and not deviated. Taking refuge in the Sangha means being pure and not polluted. These are the Three Jewels of True Nature for our practice: awakening, proper understanding, and purity. From now on, we need to forget our past and return to and rely upon these Three Jewels and use them to correct our thoughts, speech, and behavior. BACW

245. Once we attain enlightenment, we attain everything. Therefore, no matter which method we choose, the key to success is concentration on one method. So long as we adhere to our chosen method, we will achieve deep concentration, attain wisdom, and uncover the True Nature of Great Perfection.

From all of this, we can see how important the Triple Jewels are to us, for monks and nuns are the treasure of the Sangha. We need to respect all of them. We can learn from the good ones, as well as from those who do not follow the rules and guidelines. We emulate the former and use the latter to serve as negative examples.

If we fail to understand that taking refuge in the Three Jewels does not mean following a certain person, then there will be the most serious of consequences, as we will fall into Avici Hell. Why? There is only one Sangha in the universe and the Sangha in our world is a part of this whole. If we take refuge in and follow only one individual monk or nun, regard that person as our only teacher, and refuse to respect others, we will be "splitting and sowing discord among the group." This is the fifth of the Five Deadly Offenses. The first four are patricide, matricide, intentionally causing a Buddha to bleed, killing a bodhi-sattva or an arhat. Thus, it would be even worse to choose only a certain monk or nun for refuge than not to take refuge at all.

Furthermore, we only need to take refuge once. It does not accomplish anything to take refuge from one person this time and then from another later. We may think that we can get much more protection if we follow many monks and nuns. But as the saying goes: "A clay idol crossing a river cannot even protect himself." Nobody can protect us. Only when we take refuge in the Three Jewels of True Nature, can we protect ourselves. BACW

246. The Three Jewels in our true nature are awakening, correct understanding and purity. The Buddha signifies the awakening of our true nature, the Dharma signifies the correct understanding of our true nature, and the Sangha signifies purity of our true nature. We should be respectful to them. Every day, in our every thought we should ask ourselves if we are awakened? Do we have correct understanding? Are our thoughts and views correct? Are our minds pure? The purpose of dwelling in and uphold-

ing the Three Jewels is to constantly remind us of the Three Jewels of True Nature. EILS

Five Precepts

247. I met with Zhangjia Living Buddha once a week. He often reminded me, either intentionally or unintentionally, "Precepts are very important." After he passed away, I stayed by the crematory that was built especially for his cremation for three days. During those three days and nights, I kept thinking about what he had taught me for the three years that I studied with him.

Surprisingly, what made the deepest impression was "Precepts are very important." I could not figure out why but thought that there must be a reason for Master Zhangjia to keep telling me to pay attention to precepts. So I studied precepts. And then I realized that worldly rules needed to be constantly amended to suit the people of that time period. Precepts are supramundane rules, not worldly rules. If you want to transcend this world, the Six Paths, and the Ten Realms, you have to abide by precepts. AS

248. Precepts are rules that all Buddhas and bodhisattvas abide by in their cultivation over countless lifetimes. They are rules for transcending the Six Paths

and the Ten Realms, not worldly rules for daily life. That is why they cannot be changed, the Five Precepts in particular. Do you think that the Five Precepts can be changed? Is no killing wrong? How about no stealing, no sexual misconducts, no lying, and no drinking? They cannot be changed. They are major precepts by principle and indeed transcend time and space. AS

249. The Five Precepts are no killing, stealing, committing sexual misconduct, lying, and taking intoxicants. The first four offenses are physical transgressions of the true nature. Whether or not we have taken the precepts, it is wrong to commit these acts. But for one who has formally taken the Five Precepts, this will be considered as committing a double violation.

Taking intoxicants is different. A person who has not taken the precepts is not guilty when drinking, however, a person who has taken the precepts and then drinks will have broken this precept. The purpose of refraining from intoxicants is to prevent us from committing the first four transgressions while under the influence; therefore, intoxicants in themselves are not wrong. This is an example of why we need to understand the purpose of the Buddha's precept setting, its function, and its benefit. BACW

250. The Buddha taught the basic Five Precepts and the first of these is the first of the Ten Good Karmas: do not kill. Continuing to kill is to completely disregard his teachings and is an ultimate act of disrespect. This disrespect is tantamount to being unfilial to our parents. Consequently, if we ignore these instructions and kill, we are neither compassionate nor filial. BACW

251. When we practice adhering to the precepts, the most important point is to follow their fundamental spirit; "Do nothing that is bad: do everything that is good." Doing nothing bad is a Theravada precept directed toward us and is to be followed conscientiously in order to develop self-discipline. The Chinese call this "Attending to one's own moral wellbeing even while alone." When we practice self-discipline, we need to remain true to the precepts, even when no one is around. "To do all that is good" is for the benefit of all beings and is a bodhisattva precept that teaches us

how to interact with others. Precepts are the criteria for distinguishing between good and bad. BACW

252. Some people have complained that there are too many precepts, that it is too easy to violate them, and thus, they abandon abiding by them. This is why most people prefer reading or listening to talks about the sutras while avoiding those on precepts. We need to remember that precepts guide us in our behavior and are the proper conduct of all Buddhas. If there were no precepts, there would be no Buddhism. If there were no courtesies, there would be no Confucianism. Merely reciting the sutras without practicing their teachings will result in our not receiving any of their benefits. BACW

253. A good illustration [of living a simple life] is my late teacher, Mr. Li Bingnan, who lived a simple yet happy life. For decades, he only ate one meal a day, but, whenever he was invited out for dinner, he accepted. On several occasions, he invited me to accompany him. Since I had been practicing the precept of not eating after noontime for years, I felt very uncomfortable when being invited.

Mr. Li simply said, "Come with me! Come with me!" Later he explained: "With this attachment, you will not be able to help people because if you intend to help them, you must help them to be happy. Eating this dinner is not violating the precepts but lifting them. They invited you with good intentions. If you reject their invitations, they will think you are closed to reason. Then, they will not only reject Buddhism; but, will also say that we practitioners are arrogant and look down upon others. They may also urge others to avoid Buddhists. So, you could ruin the opportunity of an untold number of people to learn of Buddhism. This will result in the creation of negative karma for you."

Therefore, he was not violating the precepts but was instead simply lifting them for this meant making others happy, helping them to learn of Buddhism as well as according with conditions. . . .We can see from this that Buddhism is flexible. BACW

Paramitas

254. When we are willing to let go of our wealth, we will gain wealth. When we give teachings, we will gain wisdom. When we give fearlessness, we will gain health and long life. The law of causality is a reality and as natural as the laws of heaven and earth. If we perform goodness without expectation of reward, without the wish for prestige, wealth, wisdom, health, or long life, without the wish for anything, then we are bound to uncover everything that is already in our true nature. Is this not being free and having great contentment? CD

255. The first paramita is giving. For us, this means letting go and helping others. There are three kinds of giving: the giving of wealth, the giving of teachings, and the giving of fearlessness. Giving is a karmic cause. If we want to have wealth, we should practice the giving of wealth. If we want to be intelligent and wise, we should practice the giving of teachings. If we wish to have good health and a long life, we should practice the giving of fearlessness.

In the giving of fearlessness, the most important thing is not to harm any being. In addition to not killing beings, we should not even cause them to have afflictions. A vegetarian diet is a form of the giving of fearlessness: We do not eat the flesh of animals or cause them to have afflictions. To be more proactive, we should free captured animals. EILS

256. The second paramita is abiding by the precepts. We should observe the precepts and codes of behavior that the Buddha laid out. The teachings in the sutras that the Buddha earnestly and patiently taught us should be followed too. We should also abide by the laws and customs of our countries. If we abandon the precepts, then the practice and upholding of the Buddha's teachings will disappear. EILS

257. The third paramita is patience. To accomplish any undertaking, one needs to bear any hardship that one encounters. In the process of cultivation, one will surely encounter frustration. The more diligent one is, the greater the amount of frustration one faces.

Why is there so much frustration? Because of the evil karmas that one has committed over countless kalpas, obstacles from karmic forces are unavoidable. The only solution is to tolerate any hardship. This will decrease karmas. If one has meditative concentration, it can eliminate karmas. One should face obstacles with wisdom, resolve them with forbearance, acquiesce, and make diligent progress. Only with the paramita of patience will one be able to improve. If one is not patient, one will encounter obstacles. EILS

258. The fourth paramita is diligence. The Chinese term for "diligence" is *jingjin*. Jing means "pure and unadulterated" and jin means "making progress." For bodhisattvas, diligence is the only virtuous root.

Nowadays, many Buddhist practitioners make the mistake of learning too many different things, resulting in a mixture. Although they make progress every day, their progress is adulterated. They spend a lot of time and effort but their accomplishment is very limited.

The little achievement I have in this lifetime is due to having a good teacher. He forbade me to proceed in an unfocused and random way. I learned from Mr. Li Bingnan in Taichung for ten years.

His teaching method was that even if a student was very smart and had an exceptional capability, he or she could simultaneously only learn two sutras at most. If the student wanted to learn three sutras [at one time], he would not teach this student. Students who did not have a good capability learned only one sutra.

Only when Mr. Li considered that a student had learned a sutra well enough would he teach the student a new one. Otherwise, he would not allow the student to learn a new sutra. During my ten years with Mr. Li, I learned five sutras, whereas in a Buddhist college, the students study more than five sutras in one semester. EILS

259. The fifth paramita is meditative concentration. It means being in control of one's mind. Within, the mind is unmoved; without, the mind is not attached to phenomena. One should not be easily tempted by any external phenomena. For example, when one learns a sutra, one concentrates on this sutra. This way, one would be in control of one's mind. EILS

260. The sixth paramita is wisdom. Simply put, when one interacts with people and engages in tasks, one should do so based on reason, not on emotions. EILS

261. Are adverse encounters good for us? For practitioners, yes! It is good training to have someone constantly causing trouble for us and to not have things going our way. Without these adversities, how would we achieve concentration? Adverse conditions and affinities provide us with just the right opportunities to discipline ourselves and to practice the Paramita of Patience. We cannot be thankful enough for these opportunities, much less to complain about them or get angry. CD

Amitabha Village

262. Presently, there are only a few countries that provide social welfare for their senior citizens. Countries such as the United States and especially Australia have complete social welfare programs, and seniors are very well taken good care of.

But retirement organizations, whether run by the government or by the private sector, mostly emphasize caring for seniors' physical conditions and pay less attention to enriching their spiritual life. Those who take care of the seniors often do so mechanically and may show little love or consideration. Consequently, seniors can feel empty, lonely, and helpless, waiting daily for death.

In view of this and inspired by the four kinds of mind and practice of great compassion that we learn in the *Avatamsaka Sutra*, I have a new idea for senior retirement. I hope people of vision and foresight will gladly promote and implement it. Seniors have devoted themselves to society and should start enjoying good fortune in their old age. This is the realization of a perfect society. MT

263. Every one of us has parents, and most of us will also become old some day. Mencius said, "We should respect our parents and extend that respect to all old people; we should love our children and extend that love to all children."

Seniors have dedicated their lives to their families, society, and countries. It is only appropriate that children show filial piety to their now elderly parents and repay their kindness. We should truly extend the filial piety for our parents to all the seniors in the world, establish a paradise for seniors, and show our love and respect for them.

If we can do so and, additionally, (1) help religious groups and ethnic groups to work together, (2) propagate good traditional cultures in the world, and (3) promote the sages' teachings of filial piety, respect for those who are older, and loving-kindness, then all people will be happy and they will support our undertaking, together with the beings from all dimensions. A harmonious world can be expected soon. MT

Interfaith Harmony and Multiculturalism

264. The Buddha's teaching, the teaching of all the sages throughout history and around the world, and religious teaching all are multicultural education. In particular, the *Avatamsaka Sutra*, which is a summary of Buddhism, truly contains profound wisdom from the perfect fusion of different religions and cultures.

For example, all the organs of a body, such as the eyes, the ears, the nose, tongue, hands, and feet, must do their duties and cooperate with other organs. This way, the body will be healthy.

All of the ethnic groups, cultures, religions, schools of thought were originally a single life community. Therefore, they should seek common ground and put aside differences, exist and flourish side by side, respect and help one another, get along harmoniously, and treat one another equally. The universe was originally harmonious. The world was originally one family. MT

265. Religious respect and cooperation is the foundation for global harmony. To achieve world peace,

there must be harmony and equal treatment among countries, among political parties or political factions, among ethnic groups, and among religious groups.

It is difficult to achieve this, but it is easier to start with achieving harmony among religious groups. Religious respect and cooperation must be based on learning from each other in order for one's own religions to stay vital. If every religious adherent were able to practice the teachings of the sages—compassion, loving-kindness, sincerity, respectfulness, humility, and harmony—and get along harmoniously with others and treat them equally, then perfect harmony and social harmony would be near. MT

266. The core of the teachings of all sages, in this world and beyond, is sincere loving-kindness. Through the teaching of morality, the law of cause and effect, wisdom, and science, the sages aim to uncover the virtue of the utmost purity and virtuousness innate in all sentient beings. These virtues will manifest when interacting with others and engaging in daily tasks. MT

267. Today, many religious scholars believe that God or a deity has no physical body; He is omnipresent. This statement also applies to Dharma-nature in Buddhism. Therefore, we know that although different terms are used, all religions speak of the same thing.

I have discussed this basic concept with many religious leaders, and we all agree that the gods worshipped in all religions are the one and only true God in the universe. I asked them, "Do you agree that the true God has perfect wisdom?" They agreed. "The true God has miraculous powers, which are inconceivable, and can transform into anything." They believed this.

And then I said, "He has turned into Sakyamuni of Buddhism, Confucius of China, Jesus Christ of Christianity, and Prophet Muhammad of Islam. All these people were in fact the true God. Therefore, we are all family."

It is admirable of these religious leaders to accept this idea with open hearts. I thought that a lot of discussion might be required before they would accept this idea, but it has been warmly received by my religious friends. This is quite rare and commendable. LS

268. To resolve conflict and promote social stability and world peace, we have to stop competing for recognition and material gain, and actively promote the teaching of benevolence, justice, and compassion, a teaching that will help all beings attain enlightenment. This teaching is the same as the teaching of love taught in religion: God loves people.

Through careful observation, we will really appreciate that all the great sages in every country throughout time and the founders of the major religions, who were all sages, completely renounced material gain and greed, and had pure minds. Therefore, they practiced what they taught and were able to teach others to practice. They exerted far-reaching influence during their times and on future generations. LS

269. The goal of religious education is to realize the truth of all phenomena, which the earth, the heavens, and I originate from. All things and I are one, not two.

The effect of the religious education is to reach complete virtue and ultimate wisdom, respect all beings, and vow to serve all beings.

From this we can understand that religious education is the guideline to realizing a harmonious society and a happy life. If we pay attention only to rituals and fail to profoundly comprehend the essence of the sutra's teaching, we will not progress any further than just being zealous about our faith and thus be easily manipulated by those with bad intentions. REN

270. The Qur'an says that Allah is benevolent. The Bible says: "For God so loved the world . . . ." The foundation of Confucius' and Mencius' teaching is benevolence, righteousness, loyalty, and forgiveness. The goal of Mahayana Buddhism is sincerity and compassion.

Therefore, we can understand the goals of all religions in this world are benevolence, compassion, universal love, sincerity, respect, humility, and harmony. The content of all religions include these five teachings: ethics, morality, causality, philosophy, and science. The first three categories are universal teachings for all people regardless of gender, age, or social status. All people should learn these teachings in earnest. The latter two categories are fields of teachings, which are deeply studied by a few individuals. REN

271. We start with the training of teachers by establishing an institute of religions. After that, we establish a university of religions or a multicultural university where these teachers can go on to teach students.

To train outstanding propagators, courses in morality, virtues, religious texts, the law of cause and effect, science, philosophy, and so on should be conducted. Each religion should establish its own college. Each college has both compulsory courses and specialized courses. In addition to focusing in the texts of his or her religion, a student can also study the teachings of other religions.

After being assessed and endorsed by the government as being truly beneficial to social harmony and stability, lectures can be broadcast to religious adherents throughout the entire country and even around the world via the Internet and satellite television. MT

272. Founders of all religions were actually the different forms and identities that the true God took for the purpose of teaching diverse ethnic groups, with their varied cultural and historical backgrounds, at different times. Though the teaching methods are different,

when we look at them carefully, we will see that their directions, goals, and purposes are the same.

The starting point of all religions is love. That the starting point is the same means that they share the same goal and direction. Therefore, religious groups can work together. There were nine religious groups in Singapore while I was there. They really worked together as one and got along harmoniously like brothers and sisters. This helped to bring stability and peace to the country. LS

273. Our true nature is neither physical nor spiritual, nor a natural phenomenon. It is true purity, true goodness, compassion, impartiality, and perfect enlightenment. True nature neither arises nor ceases. It is all-knowing and able to create everything without confrontation.

Everything, no matter how insignificant, is derived from their own original true nature. It is referred to as the true creator of the universe, the true God in many scriptures of different faiths and religions. We should realize that we are unified into God all the time (not just "with God"). We are unified into the universe as oneness. The world is created by the power of consciousness. RRE

274. Religious harmony is the key to world peace. If each religion can promote impartiality and strive to attain harmonious coexistence, then harmonious relationships among 1) countries, 2) ethnic groups, and 3) political factions can be achieved. Moreover, religious harmony is the easiest to begin with when compared to the other three relationships, because all religious texts teach us to do good deeds and abandon evil deeds, to let go of selfishness, to enhance our spirits, and to refrain from pursuing wealth, fame, and other selfish desires. If religious adherents truly practice what the sacred texts teach, the adherents will live in harmony with all beings. RRE

275. The ultimate goal of the teaching of all religions is to guide the human mind to goodness. Therefore, a religion should take up the mission of righting the human mind and eliminating disasters. There are more people who have a faith than those who do not. If those who have a faith can take the lead, restoring the sages' teaching of morality, virtues, and causality,

and, starting from themselves, truly practice the teaching of the sages, they will be able to move those who do no have a faith. Through this, they can lead their countries, political parties, and ethnic groups to return to harmony—harmony in having the same understanding and in sharing benefits— and to where people get along harmoniously, treating one another equally. This way, world stability and harmony can be achieved. SC

276. In striving for eternal happiness, we must eradicate all that is bad and embrace all that is good to transform delusion into enlightenment. It is important to be virtuous in our thoughts and conduct, and to live in harmony with people of all races, religions, and nationalities, and with all beings. If we regard all seniors as our parents and all children as our own as we care for, protect and guide them, we will be setting good examples. Thus, we will attain peace and happiness for all. AL

277. All the religions in the world, however diverse, are of one family and originally lived in harmony with each other. As the name of the *Avatamsaka Sutra* im-

plies, in a garden there are various species of magnificent flowers, each showing their unique beauty and fragrance, together creating a beautiful scene. But if the garden is limited to only one species, isn't it boring? RRE

278. To help people develop confidence in religious education, every religion should establish their own model cities of harmony. Through constant teaching, the teachings in the sacred texts will be practiced in daily life. This will inspire other cities to follow suit. As a result, the whole country will be stable and peaceful, and people will enjoy happiness. Eventually, the whole world will be led to harmony. This will be the greatest contribution of religious education to today's society. I believe that this sacred undertaking will have the help and blessing from the sages of all the religions. SC

279. Why is love regarded as the core of the sacred teachings? The reason is that the universe is created by an exclusive creator, the noumenon of the universe, who dominates all in the universe. Humans are cer-

tainly inclusive. The creator therefore is also the noumenon of humankind.

Since we are integrated into all beings in the universe, we should love everybody and every object the
same as we love our own bodies (externally, the five
sense organs; internally, the organs of the body).
Catholics and Christians call the noumenon of the
universe "God," Muslims say "Allah," Buddhists say
"true nature," and Taoists say "Tao." Although it is
called something different by each religion, the essence is the same. For example, the Bible says: "In the
beginning was the Word, and the Word was with
God, and the Word was God." (John 1:1 NAB). RRE

280. Particularly in this age, when information is
readily available, the whole world has become a village. If religious adherents truly learn their religious
texts, they will appreciate the wondrous meaning of
"There is only one true God and the truth is eternal
and unchanging." For example, the omniscient and
omnipotent God has hundreds or thousands of manifestations. He is called Allah in Islam and God in
Christianity and Catholicism. He manifested as Confucius, Mencius, Laotzu, and Zhuangtzu in China. In

Buddhism, he is called the true nature. All the different terms were created to accord with the different historical and cultural backgrounds of the beings and to facilitate teaching. BC

281. Religious groups should work together and help each other. In addition, they should learn from each other and show the love of the sages through those of us who have a faith. We should start from the religion we believe in. We should broaden our minds, love our religions as well as all other religions. We learn not only the sacred texts of our religion but also those of other religions. We will further understand that all religions are truly one family. The core of the teaching of all religions is nothing but compassion and loving-kindness. SC

282. Today, travel and communication are more convenient. Religions should have more interaction with each other, cooperate with and learn from one another. We should understand the teachings given by the true God to the different religions and thus deepen our understanding of our own religious texts. We should bring ourselves closer to the true God.

Most importantly, religious adherents should express the love of God by their actions, by propagating it to people all over the world and thus saving the world. RRE

283. On the basis of religious cooperation, we should take the next step to promote mutual learning among religions in order to strengthen the spirits of unity. Mutual learning will enable us to realize that there is only one true God in the universe. All the holy ones of different religions are the manifestations of the one true God.

We should understand that all the sacred teachings are literally given by the one true God but in different forms or appearances. Therefore, I respect all the holy Gods of the different religions. In reality, I am respecting one true God. By studying all religious texts, we can deepen our understanding of the teachings of the same true God. By doing so, we can bring ourselves closer to God, enhance our spirits, broaden our minds, encompass all in the universe, and bring ever-lasting peace and harmony to all beings. RRE

284. All of the different religions in the world are one family. We should completely let go of arrogance, jealousy, and greed, treat one another equally, get along with everyone harmoniously, and work together to help people awaken. Suffering arises from delusion. Happiness arises from awakening. Only when we are truly awakened will we naturally leave suffering behind and attain happiness. OH

285. Our true nature is neither physical nor spiritual. It is true purity, true goodness, compassion, impartiality, and universal love. True nature neither arises nor ceases. It is all-knowing and able to create everything without confrontation. In various religions, people refer to this as the true creator of the universe, the true God. SE

286. For years, I have diligently learned various religious texts such as the Old and New Testaments and the Qur'an. When I study the Bible, I become a devout Christian or a devout Catholic. When I study the Qur'an, I become a devout Muslim. My sincerity and respect for Allah and God are pure and impartial, just like my sincerity and respect for Buddhas and bodhi-

sattvas. I deeply understand that only when I completely put down the three obstacles of jealousy, anger, and greed, and affirm that all sages are my best teachers will I benefit from studying the texts and really understand the true meanings of the sages' teachings. SE

287. I deeply believe that religious teachings on causality, morality, and ethics will definitely turn the bad in us humans to good, pollution to purity, and delusion to enlightenment. This is the only correct solution to various kinds of conflicts and human and natural disasters. If the adherents of diverse faiths and religions can cooperate sincerely; observe the rules; cultivate themselves; practice the teachings and influence others; learn from one another; respect one another; love, care about, and cooperate with one another; then society and the world will be harmonious. RRE

288. If we want to save the world today, religions must have solidarity and mutually coexist and cooperate in both good times and bad. In order to achieve religious cooperation and solidarity, we must take religious education as the foundation, and every relig-

ious adherent should learn his or her own sacred texts in depth. Also, we should learn from one another, respect our differences, and seek common ground. Doing so, the effect of religious cooperation will be long lasting and continuously vibrant. REN

289. If we want to truly achieve social stability, harmony, and prosperity, we should start with education. Religious prayers only effect a temporary solution, not a permanent cure. To effect a permanent cure requires transforming the human mind and helping everyone abandon evil and cultivate goodness, amend their conduct, and set their thoughts upright. We should earnestly and diligently implement religious education and propagate it. If every religion can engage continuously in teaching for years, this will be of great help to eliminate disasters and promote harmony. SC

290. If one sincerely follows the teaching, one will gain the true benefit, no matter what teaching it is, be it Confucianism, Buddhism, or Taoism, or any other religion. It is because all religions have their own fundamental precepts. If any practitioner truly realizes the precepts of his religion in daily life, he will natu-

rally be peaceful and tranquil. If we don't learn from the fundamental teachings, the whole learning process would be like a tree without roots, like water without a source, like flowers in a vase, like a house built on empty air. We will only have academic accomplishments. The practitioner will hardly be a person who will alleviate suffering, change delusion into enlightenment, and transform ordinary beings into saints and sages. REN

291. For the purpose of facilitating teaching, Buddhism divides the entire universe into three parts: noumenon, mind, and matter. These three parts are actually one entity. Noumenon is the essence, which is considered by Buddhism to be able to manifest and alter phenomena. In the statement "[phenomena are] manifested by the mind and altered by the consciousness," the mind is the noumenon, and the consciousness refers to discrimination and attachments, both of which manifest everything in the universe.

That which can be manifested and the manifested are one, not two. From here, we try to understand that the entire universe is oneself. Our minds merge with Dharma-nature, and our bodies merge with

Dharma-body. Dharma-body refers to the physical phenomena in the universe, and seeing, smelling, cognition, and knowing refer to the mental phenomena in the universe. These two kinds of phenomena come from the same origin. This origin is called Dharma-nature in Buddhism and is called God or deities in other religions. LS

292. I have long admired the traditional Chinese cultures of Confucianism, Buddhism, and Taoism, as well as the sacred teachings of different religions in the world. Even with fifty-nine years of learning, I often feel that I have much more to learn. I never tire of learning and I'm always eager to share what I've learnt with others. Now I am eighty-four years old, and I still take great pleasure in learning. I never feel that I am too old to learn. SE

293. As long as we have a pure, kind, sincere, and compassionate minds, then there will be world peace, and the surrounding environment will become beautiful. But if we have impure minds, with thoughts of benefiting ourselves while harming others, and if we have many ill thoughts of greed, anger, ignorance, and

arrogance, we will bring forth many disasters, as what is happening in the world right now. In other words, we reap exactly what we sow. The chapter "The Instruction of Yi" in the *Book of History* states: "Do good and a hundred good fortunes will manifest. Do evil and a hundred misfortunes will ensue." The Qu'ran states: "And whatever of misfortune befalls you, it is because of what your hands have earned." (42:30, Noble Quran) The Bible states: "Is it not calamity to the unrighteous, And disaster to the workers of iniquity?" (Job 31:3 ASV) MC

294. All the founders of all religions voluntarily taught multicultural teachings. For example, Jesus taught for three years, the Prophet Muhammad taught for twenty-seven years, and Buddha Shakyamuni taught for forty-nine years. Every day, they all set perfect examples with their own conduct. Their behavior was sincere and compassionate, even when they were still or silent.

Therefore, religious adherents should deeply realize that religious education is necessary for a harmonious world. If we fulfill our responsibilities in whatever position we are in and put into practice the teachings on ethics, morality, and causality, and cultivate ourselves to teach others, I believe a utopian world can be expected soon with religions coexisting in good times and bad. REN

295. [I was once asked by a student,] "How can different religious groups get along harmoniously without conflict?" I answered that the most important thing is to learn one's own religious teaching diligently.

For example, Indonesia acknowledges five religions: Islam, Catholicism, Christianity, Hinduism, and Buddhism. These five religions are like a person's five fingers. They differ in length, but when one traces them back to the palm, the wrist, and the arm, one will know that the fingers share the same root and the same origin.

Therefore, as long as one continues to delve deeply into one's religious texts, when one gets to a certain level, one will naturally comprehend the teaching. When one is exposed to the texts of other religions, one will also be able to understand them. An ancient saying speaks of "delving deeply into one teaching and immersing oneself in it for a long time." When one delves deeply and reaches a certain level, one will attain a pure mind and will naturally have a thorough understanding. OH

296. When we pay close attention to the teachings in the sutras or religious texts, we will find that the spirit of the teachings and the principles taught by the sages of all religions are about 80 percent similar. The differences arise due to the sages having accommodated people's living habits and using expedient means to facilitate their teaching.

From this, we can see that the teaching of the sages originated from the true nature of all beings. The true nature originally contains every good quality and can manifest all phenomena. Everything that accords with the true nature will flourish. Anything that goes against the true nature will decline. This is why every dynasty in China passed down the sages' teachings. This way society had peaceful and stable times and people were happy. BC

297. When we carefully look at history, it is easy for us to see that the teaching of every religion in the world is a perfect multicultural social teaching of the

utmost virtuousness. The founders of all the religions were voluntary multicultural social educators.

Jesus taught for three years. The Prophet Muhammad taught for twenty-seven years. Confucius taught for five years. Sakyamuni Buddha taught for forty-nine years. They all let go of prestige, wealth, and greed completely. They were pure in mind and body. They engaged in cultivation and taught people from all walks of life, without discrimination. Therefore, they were able to exert profound and wide-reaching influence on people of their times and later generations. OH

298. The Buddhist sutras state: "All phenomena arise from our minds; our environment can be transformed by the mind." Therefore, I deeply believe that among all the religious teachings, the teachings of causality, morality, and virtue can truly transform people from evil to good, from contaminated to pure, and from deluded to awakened. These teachings are also the only way—the only proper path—to resolve all the conflicts, disasters, and calamities in the twenty-first century. If people of all religions can cooperate and work together, follow the commandments and precepts, cul-

tivate themselves, practice the teachings of their own faith and help others, learn from and respect and care for one another, then a harmonious society and peaceful world can be perfectly realized. LP/J

299. This is a multicultural world. There are different religions, schools of thought, ethnic groups, and nations. We are all part of a bigger family. How can we fight with one another? We need to live in peace while respecting individual differences. We have to respect one another. We do not ask for respect from others but respect others first. Even if there is no respect in return, we still show our sincere respect to others.

Eventually, one day others will pay their respect to us. I pay my respect to him, care about him, care for him, and help him with all my heart without asking anything in return because I know we are one entity. I know the whole universe is one entity. He just doesn't know it yet because he is still unenlightened. When he attains awareness, he will think and do the same. WPH

300. Today's world emphasizes multiculturalism and seeks cooperation among different religions, ethnic

groups, and countries. We are one entity. We need to respect, love, care about, care for, and cooperate with one another. We need to pursue harmony. How? Harmony begins within ourselves. Instead of asking others to respect and get along with us, we ourselves need to respect and get along with others first. It does not matter whether others pay equal respect to us or try to get along with us. Eventually we will move them and influence them if we persevere in respecting them.

If I have the merest thought of demanding that others first get along with me, harmony can never truly be achieved. It is because I place myself in a conflicting position with the thought of demanding, dominating, and possessing others. So I do my utmost to love other people, care about and for them, and help them wholeheartedly. I do all this without asking anything in return because I know that we are one and that this universe is one living entity. SE

Education

301. Good teachers are genuinely compassionate, kind, patient in teaching, dedicated, and try to protect their students from contamination of the mind. It is crucial for us to be close to a good teacher; however, being close does not mean being next to the teacher but rather to listen to and follow their teachings. It is usually very hard to find the right teacher and we only meet him or her after many lifetimes. Some people have said to me that I was most fortunate to have met good teachers, but where could they find one? This teacher is to be encountered rather than sought and the chances for this are rare indeed. It is a matter of affinity and the right conditions maturing. We need to nurture the good root and opportunities. BACW

302. There is a passage in "Duke Wen of Teng, Part I" in *Mencius*: A human must behave like a human. If one is well fed and warmly clad and lives comfortably but does not receive moral education, then one is no different from an animal and tends to act on impulse.

The sages (the sages here refer to Kings Yao and Shun, who lived 4500 years ago) were worried about this. King Shun appointed Xie as Minister of Education to teach people "a natural love between parents and children, mutual obligations between leaders and their people, distinct responsibilities for husbands and wives, a natural order between the old and the young, and trust between friends." This passage explains how the educational system in China was formally established. BC

303. When the teacher thinks that we are good students, he will require us to follow three restrictions; first, he will cover our eyes and block our ears so that no worries will intrude. When we truly have abandoned all attachments and gained wisdom, we will be allowed to study other methods. Therefore, extensive learning is conducted in the second stage rather than at the beginning.

Difficulties can arise if we engage in extensive learning at the very beginning. It is similar to hearing instructions from one teacher and beginning to follow him or her and then hearing instructions from a second teacher and feeling as if we were facing two paths going in different directions. With three teachers, we will be caught at a three-way junction and with four;

we are stuck at a crossroads not knowing which way to go.

Therefore, it is important to follow only one teacher at one time. BACW

304. The Buddha taught us to believe in a good teacher. We must have confidence in this good teacher. If not, he cannot help us, no matter how great his wisdom or abilities are. Do we believe that the Buddha has ultimate perfect wisdom, virtues, and abilities? Those who believe and understand have numerous and deep good roots, which were planted in past lifetimes.

My confidence in Buddhism grew as I studied and practiced it. When I first started, I had many doubts but fortunately I had good teachers who patiently and skillfully taught me. Therefore, in teaching, the most crucial thing is the teacher's attitude. ASC

305. Buddhist education is different from modern education in terms of concepts and methods; for instance, in a university we must be very careful and take our time choosing our major. Buddhism, however, is different because here we are expected to

awaken to perfect, complete wisdom first and then in the future we will become knowledgeable in all other departments of the university. Where do we start? We start from the intensive study of a certain method; as is said: "awakening in one sutra means awakening in all sutras." What does awakening mean? Awakened means we have attained wisdom. BACW

306. The innate nature of humanity is filled with purity and goodness. People seek eagerly to have a harmonious society and community. Most simply do not know the method to achieve this. Once a way is found, hope is within sight, most people are willing to do their best to see it realized. People can be easily taught. They can be taught to become better. MC

307. Modern education is similar to building a pyramid. We read extensively and then narrow the scope of learning to specialize in one subject to progress from extensive to intensive learning. But, no matter how tall the pyramid or how large its base; the pyramid has its zenith. Buddhism is different for it is like a tree with roots, trunk, branches, leaves, and finally fruits. An infinite process, it starts from one point, the

root, and develops into the Great Perfection of the True Nature so that eventually we understand everything.

Worldly knowledge has its limitations after which there is no more to learn, but Buddhism is boundless. The wisdom of Buddhism is beyond the comprehension of average people. Buddhism may seem ordinary at the beginning, but the achievements we make later are inconceivable while worldly studies initially appear extensive and comprehensive but in the end, provide no lasting accomplishment. BACW

308. The roots of Confucianism, Buddhism, and Taoism are *Guidelines for Being a Good Person* [*Di Zi Gui*], the *Ten Virtuous Karmas Sutra*, and the *Accounts of Request and Response*, respectively. I think the *Ten Virtuous Karmas Sutra* carries the same weight as the Buddhist Canon.

Why? Because the *Ten Virtuous Karmas Sutra* is the foundation of Sakyamuni Buddha's forty-nine years of learning, practicing, and teaching. It illustrates how the Buddhist canon is put into practice in daily life, at work, and in the interactions with people. Also, *Guidelines for Being a Good Person* should carry the same weight as the Confucian texts, and *Accounts of Request and Response* the same weight as the Taoist scriptures. We should value these three roots and respect them this way. We should diligently learn and practice these three roots and then propagate and enhance them. MT

309. The first eight sentences in the *Three Character Classic* are the upmost concepts in education passed on by our ancestors from thousands of years ago. "The nature of people at birth is innately good." This sentence gives human nature a positive description. Everyone is born with virtue. Sakyamuni Buddha said: "All sentient beings are originally Buddhas." So simple and direct! You are a Buddha! Why have we now become an imperfect, worldly person? In the *Three Character Classic*, there is a great explanation that explains: "Their natures are similar; their habits are vastly different." WPH

310. Mr. Ouyang Jingwu said, "We should know that there are many expedient means in Buddhism. There is no set form." If positive teaching methods are beneficial, we use them. If negative teaching methods have

advantages, we use them too. Therefore, teaching methods in Buddhism are many and varied. They can be positive or negative. Both favorable and adverse conditions can be used for teaching purposes. There is only one goal—benefiting all sentient beings by helping them break through delusion and attain enlightenment, and to leave suffering behind and attain happiness. BACW

311. The cultural teaching of the ancient sages can bring permanent stability and peace to the whole world. The most important thing is that the people themselves should truly understand traditional culture, ending their doubt and initiating belief. Traditional culture that came from the teachings of saints and sage actually flows from the true nature of all beings, transcending time and space. Such wisdom is never out of fashion. The key to successful learning is sincerity and respect. When one is neither sincere nor respectful towards the teaching of the ancient sages, even if one reads all the books, one will not obtain any true benefit. As Confucius said, "I narrate [what the ancients said] rather than write creatively. I believe in and enjoy the teachings of the ancients." SC

312. There is no difference between our original virtue and that of Buddhas or bodhisattvas. Why are we now so different? It is because our acquired habits are different. We are polluted in our everyday lives, by our environment and by complicated affairs between people. When we are polluted, we acquire bad habits. One takes the behavior of one's company. If we stay close to saints and sages every day, we will become saints. If we stay close to immoral people all the time, we will take on their behavior and eventually become immoral people. Therefore, our ancestors realized the importance of education. So in the *Three Character Classic*, the following sentence states: "If there is no teaching, our nature will deteriorate." WPH

313. Mr. Ouyang Jingwu was a great Buddhist scholar in his times. He founded China Inner Learning College in Nanjing, where many extraordinary Buddhist practitioners, both monastic and lay, were nurtured. In 1923, he gave a speech at Nanjing Normal University titled "The Buddhadharma is Neither a Religion nor a Philosophy. It is a Modern-day Essential." BACW2

314. There are four main categories in education. These four categories cannot be separated. The first is ethical relations education. The second is moral principles education. The third is causality education, and the fourth is the education taught by the saints and sages, including religious education. If the four educations can be carried out completely, the world will be peaceful, society will be stable and secure, and people will be happy and fulfilled. If the four educations are ignored, not surprisingly, the world will be chaotic. WPH

315. The propagation of the benevolence and compassion of the sages must rely on the learner himself to put these into practice through his speech, behavior, and thoughts when interacting with others and engaging in tasks. The sages' teachings teach us to begin with changing ourselves. (For example, Confucius taught the four abandonments: abandon wandering thoughts, abandon discriminations, abandon attachments, and abandon selfishness.) If one aspires to become a sage, one must begin with resolving—from one's heart—the confrontations and conflicts with others and the external environment. This way, one

will be able to understand the true meaning of the Confucian saying "To learn, and to constantly practice what is learned [and derive benefit] is pure pleasure." MT

316. I established The Lujiang Centre of Cultural Education in my hometown, the township of Tangchi, Lujiang County, Anhui Province, China. The core of the centre's teaching is the Confucian teaching of *Standards for Being a Good Person* [*Di Zi Gui*]. The center helped the local government to propagate moral education to all people. The project started with thirty-seven teachers. They spent three months learning and practicing *Di Zi Gui*. Later on, they organized a teaching team and went into villages to teach the villagers. The teachers practiced filial piety, fraternal love, kindness, and love. Within a short few months, the social atmosphere changed for the better, proving that "human nature is originally good" and "a person can be taught to be a better person." SC

317. Today, the world is in great turmoil and people yearn for wise leadership. In order to universally benefit the world, avert imminent disasters, and re-

solve immorality and the ensuing anger and conflicts, everyone must maintain a good heart, do good deeds, say good words, and be a good person. The only way to achieve this is to make every effort to promote the teaching of great awakening and to rely on the golden maxims and teachings of the sages throughout the history and around the world. It is hoped that accord can thus be reached. MT

318. An ideal modern cultivation center should be like a school. The school itself will be like a city, like an American college town. Ten such cultivation centers, since Chinese Buddhism has ten schools, are enough for the nation. Each cultivation center should be divided into two divisions: a cultivation center, which is for practice, and a learning college, which is for teaching.

Take the Pure Land school for example. A Pure Land town could be established with a Pure Land Cultivation Center and a Pure Land Learning College.

The Pure Land Cultivation Center should focus on the practice of Buddha-name chanting. There should be many cultivation halls to accommodate practitioners practicing different forms of Buddha

Remembrance, such as Buddha Remembrance by visualization, by contemplation of an image, and by Buddha-name chanting.

The Pure Land Learning College should focus on teaching the sutras and training teachers. There should be five to ten lecture halls for lecturing on the five Pure Land sutras and one treatise. Everyone will be welcome to come listen to the lectures. MT

319. A method that has long been practiced in the Buddhist community to train lecturers of the sutras is to have students repeat their teachers' lectures. Those with good learning capabilities and good memories are chosen for training. Wisdom taught in Buddhism is different from worldly intelligence. True wisdom must be based on the foundation of precept observation and meditative concentration. Repeating the lectures of one's teacher is cultivating precepts, meditative concentration, and wisdom. The first person in Buddhist history to repeat his teacher's lectures was the Elder Ananda, who was a student and personal attendant of Sakyamuni Buddha for many years. MT

320. Buddhism is also based on the foundation of filial piety. Thus, the ritual of making offerings to ancestors and the establishment of ancestral memorial halls are highly regarded, as filial piety is the ultimate root and foundation of Chinese culture. If we are able to be filial towards parents and ancestors, able to remember our roots, then we will naturally be able to think and conduct ourselves properly and to refrain from wrongdoings. CD

321. Confucius said: "I feel delightful when I can constantly practice and realize what I have learned." This "delight" is not from the outside but from our innate virtue. It is so precious! If one can do so, this person will be healthy and long-lived, happy and satisfied. Chinese ancestors often said that it is pleasant to read and study. This happiness has nothing to do with our material life, our wealth, status, or power. This happiness is from learning and practicing the teachings of the ancient sages and saints. This is the true happiness. Therefore, Mahayana Buddhism often says "Bodhisattvas are always happy and experience joy in the Dharma." WPH

322. In ancient China, those who taught young children placed great importance on basic education. They taught filial piety, respect, and sincerity, for these are the outlines of the teachings. Thus, the child is the father of the man, for the character nurtured in our childhood will become our nature when we are grown. This provides the foundation for the nurturing of sages and virtuous people who will provide for a moral society and a wisely governed country.

Since ancient times, this has been the Chinese social tradition. The Chinese say that education is essential in establishing a new government, training its leaders, and governing its people. CD

323. The teaching of all religions is essentially about the sacred teaching of loving-kindness and compassion. The word "religion," which is *zongjiao* in Mandarin Chinese, has inspiring implications. Zong means primary, important, and venerated. Jiao means education. Therefore, zongjiao means primary education, an important teaching that is worthy of our veneration.

Religious education includes the following five categories: morality, ethics, causality, philosophy, and science. If religious education can be restored and if all religions can cooperate and work together to promote the sacred teachings to the world, we can definitely achieve world peace. Then everybody will be good and everything will be good.

Education is the only way to reconcile disasters and conflicts. Education has been and is the fundamental approach to maintaining long-lasting social stability and peace in the past and present, in the East and the West. RRE

324. Since ancient times, the Chinese way of thinking has been to accord with one's nature and innate virtues. The Chinese call it the teaching of *daode lunli* and the law of cause and effect. What is daode? In today's language, dao is the rules of nature, the order in which nature functions, and "nature is harmonious—supreme harmony." De is following the rules of nature.

For example, a year is divided into the four seasons of spring, summer, autumn, and winter. This is a phenomenon of the rules of nature. This is dao. If one's life and thinking (thinking belongs to the mental world, and body to the physical world) accord with the seasonal rules of planting in spring, growing in summer, harvesting in autumn, and storing in winter, one will enjoy good physical and mental health. Therefore, following the rules of nature and according with harmony are de.

If one violates the rules of nature and breaches harmony, one will certainly suffer from bad health and be prone to illness. So we have the definition of daode. LS

325. People around the world need to return to traditional values and strive to attain peace. How do we attain peace? Through education. The most important education is that of the family as it is the basis of all education. When a family loses it sense of unity, it affects the stability of society because families are the foundation of society. The core of a family is the husband and wife, and when spouses do not get along, society will not be peaceful. This is why Confucianism, Buddhism, and Taoism emphasize family education. AL

326. All sages have their way of doing things and they are correct in doing things that way. We should clearly observe and consider all viewpoints. Then we

will be able to uncover our wisdom and to truly learn the virtues and abilities that we should learn. It is inappropriate to say that Confucius was wrong to seek a position at the imperial court and that Sakyamuni was correct to renounce worldly attachments. Both of them were correct; they simply had different ways of doing things.

We must learn from different people to make our learning complete. If one has position or power, one should work conscientiously while maintaining a pure mind as Sakyamuni did. This way, one will achieve perfection in his undertakings. LS

327. In today's society, what is the driving force behind hard work? Wealth, fame, and prestige! Most people will do whatever is necessary to acquire these. If there were no wealth to gain, how many would be willing to work so hard? Very few! In the past, the driving force behind people's hard work was filial piety. In their mindfulness of ancestors and parents, they did their best to accumulate merits and virtues on their behalf, and to honor them. This driving force is much worthier and nobler than that of wealth, fame, and prestige! This has been the tradition of Chinese

culture and Confucian teaching for several thousand years. CD

328. Many practitioners have asked me, "Ms. Han Yin has passed away many years ago and yet you still miss her. Isn't this an attachment?" I replied that if my missing her is based on emotions, then it is an attachment, but if it is based on wisdom, then it is a teaching. I had a hall built in commemoration of Ms. Han. This is for educational purpose: teaching the public to keep in mind the favors others have done to them and to repay kindness. I always keep in mind all the favors Ms. Han had done for me and try to repay her kindness. ASC

329. Education of children should start from pregnancy. Although many parents may not try to exert good influence on their children before birth, they know that after a baby is born it will be influenced by what it sees and hears. Regardless of whether a baby is able to understand, as soon as it opens its eyes it will see and hear, and it starts learning and imitating. Doing so is its nature, and nature is dao. At this time,

the parents should exert positive influence on the baby, and this is teaching of de. LS

330. People who truly have good fortune are kind hearted, honest, and tolerant. Their speech and manner are calm and dignified. Confucius said: "Without dignity, one is unable to inspire others." Only with dignity and the ability to inspire respect are we able to effectively interact with others. CD

331. The ancient Chinese paid great attention to the teaching of the sages. The starting point of this teaching is first of the Five Cardinal Relationships: a natural love between parents and children. The love between parents and children comes from the nature, it is not taught or created by anyone. In Buddhism, it is called an innate virtue. Education teaches children to maintain this natural love throughout one's entire life. This is the basic goal of the teaching. The next step is to enhance this love.

First, parents love their children, and children are filial to their parents; elder siblings are friendly to younger siblings, and younger siblings respect elder siblings; husbands are responsible, and wives are attentive; and rulers are benevolent to their subjects, and the subjects are loyal to their rulers. Next, people should love their friends, their neighbors, their own communities and then society, their country, and the human race. "Human beings, regardless of any differences, should be loved equally." SC

332. Ancient Chinese sages were knowledgeable about science and technology, and yet they chose not to continue development of such knowledge. Why? They foresaw that in the end, technology would destroy our world. So, they chose instead to concentrate on the humanities, to help people develop wisdom, and to understand and practice morality, to help people fully understand the relationship between humans, among humans and spirits, and among humans and nature, and to become a person who is fearless and indomitable. Only in this way, will individuals experience true happiness and well being, and will citizens and countries have a genuine future. This is genuine education. CD

333. As to the importance of moral education, ancient Chinese sages particularly emphasized that for people

to enjoy happiness, families to enjoy harmony, countries to enjoy stability, and the world to enjoy peace, self-cultivation is fundamental and education is essential. To achieve these four goals, we must start with cultivating ourselves and also propagate the teachings of the sages. BC

334. What Buddhas and sages realized and gained is love for self. What they taught is love for others. The teaching of all sages is the teaching of sincerity, love, and the standards of behavior in life as enunciated in *Guidelines for Being a Good Person* [*Di Zi Gui*] and in the Ten Virtuous Karmas. The teaching of all sages is the inheritance of human wisdom and experience as well as the heritage of world civilizations. LS

335. Since ancient times, Chinese emperors and governments in all dynasties regarded teaching as their first priority. Of all the measures adopted and implemented by the government, education was the most important. All other measures supported education. BC

336. If one wishes to have good siblings or children, family education must be taught in one's family. For a family to prosper, education is essential. When one enters society, whether one runs a business or engages in an occupation, if one wishes the business to prosper, the first priority is educating the employees. BC

337. Chinese education is a teaching of benevolence and justice, love, and supreme harmony. It does not teach one to compete for material gain. Therefore, children should be taught to give precedence to others at a young age.

In addition to learning to refrain from competing with others, they should also learn to sacrifice themselves. It is different from today's education, which starts teaching competition in kindergarten. Competition denotes selfishness. When children are taught to compete for recognition and material gain at a young age and are instilled with the concept of benefiting oneself at the expense of others, as grownups they will not realize that benefiting oneself at the expense of others is wrong.

Therefore, the teaching of love teaches people to love others as they love themselves, always thinking about making sacrifices and about serving others—society, the country, and all beings. When doing so, they never consider their own interests. The teaching of the sages starts from here. LS

338. My teacher Prof. Fong Dongmei introduced Buddhism to me and said: "The Buddha is a great philosopher, a revered philosopher. Buddhism is the pinnacle of all philosophies in the world, and learning Buddhism is the greatest enjoyment of life."

With the scientific advancements in recent years, especially in the field of quantum physics, people are gradually seeing that what the Buddha said 2500 years ago was indeed a true description of the reality of the universe. By continuous and profound study of the sutras, we believe that not only will Buddhism be "the pinnacle of all philosophies in the world," it will also be recognized as the highest form of morality, virtue, causality, and science. In twenty to thirty years, Buddhism will be accepted as an advanced science. REN

339. Parents and elders must set an example for the children. Babies see and hear upon their birth. They

start to imitate others even before they can speak or walk. The speech and conduct of their elders must conform to moral principles and ethics so that what the babies see, hear, and come in contact with will influence them positively. The Chinese proverb "The behavior of a child three years old will reveal what this person will be like at the age of eighty. The behavior of a child of seven will reveal what this person will be like throughout his or her whole life" makes a lot of sense. LS

340. If we are truly awakened, we should remember the teaching of Great Master Yinguang: practice with a small number of practitioners at a small cultivation center; do not seek affinities; chant "Amituofo" single-mindedly and seek rebirth in the Western Pure Land. If an opportunity arises for us to teach students, then do so to pass down the teachings of the sages. It does not matter how many students we have; it takes only one student to pass down the teachings. ASC

341. Good advice is the teachings of the sages of this world and beyond. Later generations called these teachings sutras. The sutras speak of truths that do

not change with time. The truth that surpasses time is the same now, as it was thousands of years ago; it never changes whether in the east or in the west.

The writings and teachings of sages did not come from their personal experiences and opinions, for if they did they would be biased or inappropriate. History is not made up of opinions but of accumulated experiences whereas sutras contain the truth that arises from the original true nature. Thus, the teachings in the sutras are the absolute truth that surpasses time and space.

We will benefit and improve if we believe in the teachings, but if we do not, then we will miss these remarkable benefits. This is why we say that doubt is one of the six fundamental afflictions of greed, anger, ignorance, arrogance, doubt, and deviated views. CD

342. The first goal of ancient Chinese education was to ensure that the affection between parents and children would remain unchanged during their lifetimes. The second goal was to enhance this sincere love and to expand its scope to include the family, brothers and sisters, the community, society, the country, humankind, and even all beings. One should love not only

humankind but also animals, trees, flowers, and grass. This was the concept, and it was the desired goal of Chinese education to expand the scope of this love. LS

343. The *Ten Virtuous Karmas Sutra* is the foundation for entering Buddhism. But before one enters Buddhism, one must have the foundation of learning *Guidelines for Being a Good Person* [*Di Zi Gui*] and *Accounts of Request and Response*. *Guidelines for Being a Good Person* is the foundation of Confucian moral education. It contains teachings for family education. Parents and elders teach a child filial piety and respect for teachers. *Accounts of Request and Response* is the foundation of Taoist teaching of the law of cause and effect. BC

344. When one learns the teaching of the law of cause and effect, one will not dare to commit evil deeds. When one receives moral education, one will feel ashamed to commit evil deeds. If one has such a foundation when one enters Buddhism, it will not be hard for one to learn the Five Precepts and the Ten Virtuous Karmas. When one truly practices the teachings

in the *Ten Virtuous Karmas Sutra*, *Guidelines for Being a Good Person* [*Di Zi Gui*], and *Accounts of Request and Response*, one will truly break through suffering and attain happiness. BC

345. During his lifetime, Sakyamuni held more than 300 teaching assemblies. His teaching was very rich in content. He began teaching at the age of thirty and passed away at seventy-nine. He spent forty-nine years teaching without interruption. We know that Confucius taught for only five years, and Jesus taught for three years before he was killed. Prophet Muhammad taught for twenty-seven years. Among the ancient and contemporary sages of all ethnic groups, Sakyamuni indeed was the one who taught for the longest period of time, and the content of his teaching was the richest. Therefore, the results of his teaching are outstanding. His life provides a good example for us. Only through education can we really reconcile all conflicts that are complicated and complex. LS

346. Teaching and learning are the foundation that will lead to a harmonious world for all beings. Re-

gardless of the time or place, the root of social stability and happiness is teaching and learning. They are the only way demonstrated by all the great saints and sages. Other approaches are not the correct paths. LP/M

347. The Chinese say that education is essential in establishing a new government, training its leaders, and governing its people. If the basic quality of education is not clearly recognized and implemented, incorrect views can be destroy the entire culture, country, and even its people!

All the government officials in ancient China studied the works of wise sages and virtuous people. Even if some had selfish intentions, their wrongdoings were probably limited. They would have only bent the rules only so much before they started feeling regretful.

Today, sexual misconduct, wrongdoings, even criminal acts are all viewed as matter of fact. We no longer have a shameful heart or feel remorseful. We have lost our sense of morality and our conscience. And this is deeply troubling because all that separates us from animals is a good heart. CD

348. What children see and hear during their first three years will leave a deep impression on them, and they will be able to tell right from wrong and good from evil at the age of three. These children will be immune to many harmful pollutants in the contemporary world. This immunity will be with them from birth.

When they start attending primary school at the age of six or seven, if teachers make sure that the children adhere to moral principles and ethics every day, it will enhance and extend the moral education that the children have been receiving since birth.

This will help them form a foundation for good character, which will ensure virtuous thoughts, speech, and conduct for the rest of their lives. The children will give priority to others, treat others with respect and humility, engage in tasks with caution, and get along harmoniously with others. Therefore, no dispute will arise. After they have formed a foundation for moral conduct, they should be taught the writings of the sages to receive the teaching of ethics, morality, the law of cause and effect, and wisdom. LS

349. If society is to remain stable, its members need to live in harmony. Only harmony can draw us together in terms of opinions, ideas, and our way of life. In other words, being harmonious can minimize the differences in human relations and improve equality. After that, peace and then finally, happiness can be achieved. To obtain happiness we must have a peaceful heart and body. Both Buddhist and worldly teachings emphasize the importance of harmony and respect. BACW

350. We mutually respect, love, and cooperate with one another, setting ourselves as a model of peace and harmony to show the whole world that multi-racial, multicultural, and multifaith harmony—and peace—is achievable.

The ideal of the human race becoming one family is attainable. MC

SOURCES

Sources

AL: *Awakening of Lovingkindness*. Translated by Silent Voices. Singapore: Amitabha Buddhist Society (S), 2000.

ASC: *Amitabha Sutra* Commentary. Lecture Series given in Toowoomba, May 2003. Translated by the Pure Land Translation Team. Toowoomba. Translation currently ongoing.

BACW: *Buddhism: The Awakening of Compassion and Wisdom*. First Edition. Translated by Silent Voices. Singapore: Amitabha Buddhist Society (S), 1999.

BACW2: *Buddhism: The Awakening of Compassion and Wisdom*. Second edition. Translated by the Pure Land Translation Team. Toowoomba. To be published.

BC: "Buddhist Contributions to Resolving Social Problems." Address given at The 24th General Conference of the World Fellowship of Buddhists, Tokyo, Japan, November 2008. Translated by the Pure Land Translation Team.

CD: *Changing Destiny*. Translated by Silent Voices. Singapore: Amitabha Buddhist Society (S), 1999.

EILS: *Essence of the Infinite Life Sutra*. Lecture series given in San Francisco, August 1993. Translated by Pure Land Translation Team. Toowoomba. To be published.

LP/J: "Letter to Pope Benedict XVI, In Preparation for Malaysian Interfaith Delegation's Audience with Pope Benedict in June 2010." Translated by Pure Land Translation Team. Toowoomba: 2010.

SOURCES

LP/M: "Letter to Pope Benedict XVI." Translated by Pure Land Translation Team. Toowoomba: 2010.

LS: "Learning from Sakyamuni: Reconciling Conflict and Promoting Social Stability and World Peace Through Teaching." Address given at the Celebration of the 2550th Birth Anniversary of the Buddha, UNESCO Headquarters, Paris, France, October 2006. Translated by Pure Land Translation Team.

MC: "Building a Model City of Peace and Harmony in Toowoomba." Address given at Morality & Virtues: A Faith Perspective Forum at Toowoomba, Australia, March, 2012. Translated by Pure Land Translation Team.

MN: "A Brief Introduction of Venerable Master Chin Kung's Main Thoughts." Translated by Pure Land Translation Team. Toowoomba: Pure Land Learning College Association Inc, 2008.

MR: "The Mission of Religions to Save the World." Address given at The ACRP Executive Committee Meeting, Kuala Lumpur, Malaysia, May 2011. Translated by Pure Land Translation Team.

OH: "One Humanity, Many Faiths." Address given at Interfaith Summit for Peace and Harmony in Australia and the Asia-Pacific Region, Brisbane, Australia, February 2009. Translated by Pure Land Translation Team.

REN: "Religious Education is Necessary for a Harmonious World." Address given at The 2nd International Conference of Multi-Religious and Multi-Cultural Communication, Dacca, Bangladesh, November 2010. Translated by Pure Land Translation Team.

SOURCES

RRE: "Restore Religious Education, Pray for Enduring World Peace." Address given at World Day of Prayer for Peace, The Vatican, Rome, October 2011. Translated by Pure Land Translation Team.

SC: "Eliminating Crises Through Religious Education: Thoughts On Building a Sacred City of Religions and Culture." Address given at the World Fellowship of Buddhists Interfaith Forum, Bangkok, Thailand, May 2012. Translated by Pure Land Translation Team.

SE: "Religious Education: Saving the Earth." Address given at The 3rd World Peace Forum, Yogyakarta, Indonesia, June 2010. Translated by Pure Land Translation Team.

TVKS: *The Buddha Speaks of the Way of Ten Virtuous Karmas*. Translated by Pure Land Translation Team. Translation currently on-going.

WPH: "World Peace and Harmony: An Inspiration from Water." Address given at Water & Peace Global Forum, Shiga, Japan, March 2010. Translated by Pure Land Translation Team.

INDEX

INDEX

INDEX

INDEX

May the merits and virtues
accrued from this work
adorn the Buddha's Pure Land,
repay the Four Kinds of Kindness above,
and relieve the sufferings of those
in the Three Paths below.

May all those who see and hear of this
bring forth the heart
of understanding and compassion,
and at the end of this life,
be born together
in the Land of Ultimate Bliss.

For a list of

Amitabha Buddhist Societies

and

Pure Land Centers

please visit

www.purelandcollege.org.au

Compliments of

紐約華藏淨宗學會

Amitabha Buddhist Society of NY Inc.

41-60 Main Street, Suite 211

Flushing, NY 11355

Tel: 718-961-7299 Fax: 718-961-8039